FALL OF PR
AND RISE OF ADVERTISING

Stefan Engeseth

Copyright © 2006–2009 by Stefan Engeseth

Stefan Engeseth Publishing

+46 (0)8 651 44 54

+46 (0)704 44 33 54

www.DetectiveMarketing.com

® Detective Marketing™ is a registered trademark of Stefan Engeseth

Art direction and layout: Jonas Nilsson

Illustrations: Roland Williams, Willdesign

Illustration: Joachim Nordwall, J.Nordwall Design (page 95)

Illustration: Igor Polyakov, Hot snow (page 107)

Illustration: Cecilia Hertz, Umbilical design (page 120)

Cover photo/portrait: Thomas Svensson

Photography: Helene PE (Alexander's door handle, page 146)

English language version adapted and re-worked by Steve Strid

Proofreading and editing by Ken Neptune

Proofreading by Jack Yan

Printed: Norhaven A/S, Denmark 2009

Paper: Holmen Book

Cover paper: Invercote Creato

ISBN: 978-91-633-0777-5

Dedicated to

AL RIES

10 points that are speeding up the fall of PR

1. PR can no longer fly under the nonsense (or BS) radar. Today's smart consumers see through PR messages in the media.

2. PR agencies can no longer hide the truth. With 100 million bloggers, media is no longer "the third party", but rather, just one of many voices.

3. The PR industry is doing very little for their clients' brand strategy and clients are starting to catch on.

4. A parrot can learn to say branding and advertising, but that doesn't necessarily mean he understands what they mean. (Feel free to substitute executive for parrot…)

5. Greed and competition have driven PR agencies to sell press clippings by the kilo. The result: PR has become easier to spot as artificially generated and not an especially good bargain.

6. PR agencies love crisis management – not for the challenge, but for the money. Crisis management is a cash cow and is often sold by the same agency doing the rest of the PR.

7. With limited online savvy, PR agencies' attempts to fake their way into reputable forums often backfire. (Several agencies have already been ousted for fake postings.)

8. PR agencies are nowhere near delivering what their customers are asking for. Nine out of ten of their customers surveyed aren't sure what they're paying for.✳

9. A lack of rules and ethics often drives PR agencies to go too far. (Or maybe selling seriously ill celebrities as spokespersons for pharmaceutical company products is OK? It seems that reality is more Sicko than Michael Moore's film…)

10. Due to time restraints and competition from the Web, much of what passes for news has no credible source. Try it yourself: check the sources in the newspapers you read this week. If you can find one article with a real source, one without a profit motive, frame that article. It may be the last one of its kind.

✳*Just like PR agencies' years of "bought" studies, we have used the same unscientific methods to arrive at these figures: we interviewed a large number of PR customers over a period of two years. We've talked to a number of leading multinational companies that admit they're not quite sure what they're getting from their investment in PR.*

10 points that are speeding up
the rise of advertising

1. The Internet is starving for content; advertising no longer needs to buy expensive media to reach its target.

2. The more advertising costs, the better it sells. However, the reverse is true for PR: the more you spend, the more likely the consumer is to react negatively.

3. The advertising agency creates the strategy for the brand and works directly with top management. The PR agency doesn't.

4. New insights into the human mind and the mechanics of tribes are easier to apply to advertising than PR. PR is a one night stand in a world where people are looking for lasting relationships with their brands.

5. Old school push advertising is being replaced by pull – good advertising is becoming as important as the brand itself.

6. When the sender of the message is clear, it is easier to reach today's smart consumers with advertising. This makes it easier for companies to develop the next iPhone, Google or Harley-Davidson.

7. The advertising industry has a solid framework and its long history is full of lessons learned.

8. In our digital world, advertising reaches more consumers faster than ever.

9. Advertising has become part of the entertainment industry. Consumers are getting more sophisticated. Well-conceived, honest ads can have impact like never before.

10. There's an old saying that half of all advertising is wasted, but we don't know which half. Today, half the value of advertising is getting smart consumers to spread the word, extending the reach of the advertising into niche groups.

10 ideas to rock the world with advertising

1. Build entire branded towns – P&G City, Google Downtown.
   Living your brand means living *in* your brand.

2. Pampers should sponsor sex to increase their market.

3. Put the Nobel Prize in your iPhone

4. Give away as much as you can for free, especially entertainment.
   Use advertising to foot the bill.

5. Bring Google AdWords into the off-line world of real life –
   a simple idea that could increase Google's sales by a factor of
   99%.

6. Introduce Moon Wine! Imagine, the first-ever space buzz –
   a brand that is reborn every night.

7. Virgin Space Mall – space shopping that will build buzz in
   zero gravity. Helium-filled upside down shopping bags all over
   town would make every shopper a walking billboard.

8. Buildings as advertising monuments – build Goodyear in the
   shape of a tyre or a Whirlpool house shaped like a refrigerator
   where the entire front of the building swings open.

9. From top of mind to outer space. Markets are expanding from
   earth to space and onto new bodies of water created by global
   warming. It will be as profitable as selling life jackets on the
   Titanic when it was on its way down.

10. Today's thieves are stealing cars with advertising. They put it
    on the back window and when the driver gets out to remove it,
    the car thief jumps in and drives away. Why not turn this scam
    into an event along the lines of the MTV show *Punk'd* and turn
    it into advertising for insurance.

11. Doing the right thing at the right time is good advertising (like
    reading this book in public spaces and smiling).

Stefan Engeseth is one of Europe's most creative business thinkers and a top-ranked speaker. For more information about his books, speeches, consulting and blog go to DetectiveMarketing.com

If you like this book, spread the word. (If you don't like this book, I've just wasted more than 2 years writing it.)

Contents

Foreword by Al Ries

Dear Stefan:

I certainly would have no objections if you wrote a book entitled *The Fall of PR & the Rise of Advertising.*

Controversy is what builds brands. The more controversy the better.

Actually, I agree with you that the PR industry has not done a good job in taking the reins of brand leadership from the advertising community. Most PR people still want to wait until the advertising agency sets strategy.

Good luck in whatever direction you go.

All the best.

Al Ries, author of "The Fall of Advertising & the Rise of PR"

My letter to Al Ries:

Dear Al,

After your book *The Fall of Advertising & the Rise of PR*, we could hear how Madison Avenue gasped for air all the way to Sweden. Not many modern books have had that effect.

The advertising business had it coming: they did not develop with the market. Today, I see that the PR business is making the same mistake. They are nowhere near delivering what their clients are asking for. I therefore suggest a new book:

The Fall of PR & the Rise of Advertising

I have ideas and concepts for this new book. It could be a positive shock for Madison Avenue to learn that they are now back in the game, if they take the opportunity and make use of the tools and methods in this book.

Looking forward to hearing from you when you have the time,

Kind regards,

Stefan Engeseth
DetectiveMarketing.com

Author's preface

Al Gore's proactive movie: *An Inconvenient Truth* shocked a lot of people. *The Fall of Advertising & the Rise of PR* was also an inconvenient truth when it was published. It argued that advertising didn't build brands very well and that PR was a better way of doing it. Page after page recounted the weaknesses of advertising compared to PR. Then came the clincher: "Advertising is no longer fresh and exciting. There's just too much of it. Advertising has moved to Florida and entered its retirement years" (Ries, 2002). If that was the case back in 2002, then I'll have to start calling advertising an "ex-pensioner" (as my mentor Claes Andréasson refers to himself. Before spending five minutes in "Florida", Claes worked with super-brands such as Absolut Vodka).

The strongest argument for PR has historically been credibility. Today, the PR industry has gone so far in response to a tougher media climate and the need to show quick results, that the messages have started to sound desperate and fake.

> *"We have empirical proof that today's smart consumer*
> *sees through hidden PR messages in the media."*
>
> Professor Micael Dahlén, Centre for Consumer
> Marketing, Stockholm School of Economics

Today's consumers are smarter than ever, especially as human lie detectors. Just as in Malcolm Gladwell's book *Blink,* most of us don't need more than 2 seconds to decide what's real and what's fake (Gladwell, 2007).

The "third party", as Rise calls news and PR, delivers the truth – they make a point of reminding us that what they provide is not paid advertising. However, with cutbacks in journalistic staffing, increasingly short deadlines and pressure from bloggers, many media actors simply don't have time to check PR material.

PR's falling credibility has also hit other media channels. Once upon a time, the media delivered one consistent viewpoint, which made it easy for large corporations (who, coincidentally also happened to own the media channels). With the Internet, however, their "truth" has lost some of its control. The "third party" has been partially replaced by the many voices of Web 2.0. The global world of blogging is much harder to control than in the days when a very few voices spoke to many. Today, everyone talks with everyone else. When Fox News displayed an American flag in the background in its broadcasts, the fervent patriotism was genuine. Other media channels might as well also come out of the closet and display a flag of what is closest to their hearts – a flag for Monsanto for example. Ironically, it was Monsanto that cost Fox News a good deal of credibility in the documentary *The Corporation* in 2003. This sort of film is far from rare. Books and films by Naomi Klein and Michael Moore shed new light on the darker corners of the corporate world. Stock market figures and news programs have become nothing more than a branded store window with headlines. Even the venerable BBC broadcast the crass PR film *The Great Global Warming Swindle* (2007), a corporate hatchet job on Al Gore's film *An Inconvenient Truth*. The PR film was quickly ousted for what it was and was trashed mercilessly by the blog world. It is worth noting that if one of the most credible news sources in the world can be hoodwinked, what can we believe? Advertising is often more transparent and more straightforward than PR.

In Ries's book, the fall of advertising could also be attributed to egos, awards, profit and an artist-wannabe culture. As you can imagine, the reaction was strong as the authors themselves point out: "*This book created more controversy than any other book we've written*" (ries.com).

Beware: PR can kill!

Marketing PR relies on credibility to succeed, fitting seamlessly into the media landscape. But with success comes competition and soon the messages were becoming too obvious. At the same time, young consumers were getting better at seeing through the message. PR even managed to kill some of its clients. Literally.

PR today

A case in point: some years ago, a CEO was accused of water pollution from his factory. He invited in the media to show that this was not the case and drank a glass of water from the water outside his factory. The stunt was incredibly successful and great for the PR industry. Only one problem – he died a year later of cancer. An interesting story you probably won't be hearing anytime soon from a PR consultant with a taste for a quick fix.

The PR industry is generally far too closely connected with death. A whole *product-defence industry* has emerged, using science-for-sale to defend dangerous products using dubious research results.

> *"To create credibility for Bisphenol A (BPA)– a chemical in hundreds of products that could be harming an entire generation – they are using research from Harvard…"*
> Fastcompany.com, 2009

The result of placing these kinds of questionable reports in the media has been to hide the dangerous truth about products for years. Such was the case with tobacco, climate change, fast food, sugar and a long line of pharmaceuticals. Hiding the truth is big business for the PR industry, but is also an ocean of contaminated water. What was once hidden bubbles to the surface with increasingly greater ease in books such as *Doubt is Their Product: How industry's assault on science threatens your health* by David Michaels.

So, do I have the experience to write this book? Compared with Al and Laura Ries – no. The point, however, is not my experience, but what I have to say. Does what I write make good business sense? That is the question you should be asking yourself. Even if you work with PR, you'll probably be inspired by this book (admit it, you secretly smiled when you read that 9 of 10 PR customers don't know what they're paying for.) It doesn't matter where you live in the world, be it the US, England, France or Guatemaya (excuse me, I mean Guatemala. The Rieses renamed it in a witty and provocative way in their book).

Obviously, advertising is far from a world unto itself; it is a tool for corporations to reach their goals. By opening the corporate door to the market and letting in consumer input, advertising can play a major role in the success of a company. The purpose of this book is to open this door and encourage the rise of advertising by showing business how to move forward.

At a time when advertising is struggling with technology that literally filters it out of TV, innovation in digital media is essential in reaching today's savvy consumer. In order for advertising to be effective, your audience must not only be watching, it must also be *participating*. Walking, talking and stalking 680 companies from 38 countries at Eurobest was a good reality check for the content of this book.

At a time when our earth is under threat, people are changing. Our survival instinct is springing to life and our genes are searching for survival in various communities and tribes – a trend also explored in this book. Al Gore's film acted as a sort of wake-up call for this mindset. At the same time, we are entering a new market economy where sites such as eBay demonstrate that when a consumer buys something it is not the end of the transaction, but rather, simply a sort of ticket of admission to a long-term relationship based on sustainability. Advertising can lead a brand into a world where goods change owners, but the brand lives on through the consumer. Instead of simply increasing consumption, advertising can become a responsible citizen and build tribes that can over time, or even now, become the main media for the survival and future of the brand. What would car brands be without their loyal fans who buy the used models? They give the brands a genuineness that advertising can amplify, but not replace.

Welcome to the rise of advertising.

Stefan Engeseth, DetectiveMarketing.com™

Introduction

Maslow's (1908–1970) *hierarchy of needs* explains that our basic needs such as sleep, food and sex will always be present, but in order to cope with the times we live in, they must be adapted to consumption and social networks in order to be relevant to the 21st century.

Which do we choose? Our survival instinct tells us to save energy, which is why most people take the escalator. More people would take in advertising if it helped them on the steep stairs of life.

When the world changes, so does our world view

The way we look at the world has never changed so much, so fast. We know that we're on the Titanic with an uneasy feeling that the world could go under at any time. As early as 2050, some experts say that life on our planet as we know it will no longer be possible. Start asking around and you'll notice something a little less spectacular – increasing numbers of people are buying houseboats and houses in the mountains. The coming disasters are no longer about our grandchildren or even our children, but about us. Climate change has hit our time zone and we're looking for a plan B. Naturally, we're doing what we can. Buying green is good, but contrast that with one expert prediction that water levels could rise as much as 70 m (if we're lucky!) This would certainly change our world views overnight; not only lifestyle and behaviour, but also business. Sir Richard Branson is already exploring that mindset with space travel. If you don't believe me, click on Branson's Virgingalactic.com. Soon we will see a number of completely new trends such as leaving the planet or living out at sea.

> *Man has always made war in a fight over natural resources.*
> *Soon there will be fewer natural resources and more people*
> *than ever struggling for survival.*

The market for moving into space has enormous potential, if we can create the right mindset. My approach would be called *space therapy*. It could begin with a space hotel on earth where you can live in zero gravity. The concept could then be rolled out to other cities and eventually into space (you buy accommodations on earth that include an upgrade into space when the time is right.)

Far out, you say, but people *will* live in space in the near future. Billions are being invested. What was once considered fantasy is now attracting serious investment. People understand that if Branson is investing in it, it's probably not about charity; it's about turning a profit. Our lives have become stable and a bit museum-like. Many industries are full of big players that make it too expensive for new players to get started. Establishing a super-brand such as Coca-Cola from scratch is just too expensive today.

Today's brands, however, are built for earth, not for space. They are positioned in minds that are already crammed full. Space, on the other hand, is "Virgin" territory.

Al Ries and Jack Trout's classic book *Positioning: The Battle for Your Mind* started with a magazine article in *Advertising Age* back in 1972. Now it's time for someone to write a new seminal book called *Positioning: The*

Battle for Space. One leading researcher, Steven Pinker, is digging deep to find out how the human mind really works. In his book *The Blank Slate* (2003), Pinker raises the question if space really is so empty. One thing is for certain, just as man has gone to war over land, water and air space, so he will fight in deep space as well.

Back on earth, we can see a slightly less spacey change in our attitude towards relationships. On millions of dating profiles, for example, you can often read "In a relationship, but open for suggestions..." The same is true for modern brands; people are loyal to their brand until someone comes along with a better offer. Loyalty and performance are more closely linked than ever.

Why your brain doesn't want to think

To increase the likelihood that you like this book, I'll write it like a book you've already read. According to research, you are more likely to like something that is already familiar. In a recent lecture *Brands in the Brain* an eminent professor said:

> *"Our brains don't want to think if they don't have to. The brain already consumes 20% of the body's energy and it doesn't want to waste energy evaluating something new."*
>
> Martin Ingvar, Professor of Medicine and
> Cognitive Neurophysiology, Karolinska Hospital

When people say that advertising is brain dead, they mean that it is successful or at least *was* until the consumer smartened up. What's more, the brain prioritizes negative information before positive due to our survival instinct. This makes most ads uninteresting; we'll live anyway. The farther away from the consumer you get, the less relevant the message. This increases the motivation to create your own media channels to make the advertising message more relevant, such as the TV channels created by and for Tommy Hilfiger, Audi and Diesel.

But why not take it even further? Why not create an entire branded town for Google? New approaches succeed best when they have an older component – when a certain part of the new information is already present in the mind it simplifies acceptance. Retro design is successful for this reason; it's easier to build a new Volkswagen Beetle because the old Beetle is already there in your head. This is also the reason that most successful brands are old, some far older than anyone reading this book.

Thanks to the Internet, however, man is no longer a single mind, but rather a collective one. Modern advertising often builds its own small worlds. Take Carlsberg Beer, for example. By putting its beer in another context, Carlsberg can create a great effect. "The world would probably be a better place if Carlsberg ruled more than beer" becomes a memorable message rather than just another beer ad.

When Ogilvy created a commercial for Ford Kuga, they took away everything that you could compare with other cars. They ended up with a Ford Kuga and nothing else, an ingenious way of making the car's styling more relevant and different that it really was. Their media budget of £30 million certainly helped create its own world. Even Absolut Vodka creates its own world, an Absolut World – an Absolut Los Angeles, Absolut New Orleans or an Absolut Disco. These ads link with notions already present in the mind and are therefore more relevant for those who are already part of the message.

At the same seminar, *Brands in the Brain*, Absolut said the following about consumer insight:

> *"We refuse to communicate to everyone, even if we are*
> *a big brand. Instead, we communicate with the right*
> *people and must be relevant to just them."*
>
> Eric Näf, Director Product Innovation,
> Absolut Spirits

Maybe the bad pick-up line "Haven't we met before?" still works for that simple reason: the person already has some sort of relationship with that person, or wishes to position himself as if he did.

Building brands as buildings and towns

New York never sleeps they say. Today there are many cities like New York around the world; in fact there are over 400 cities with over 1 million inhabitants. As soon as 2015 it is estimated that there will be at least 550 (Larsson, 2009). All of these cities together account for about half of the world's population and it is often in these cities that trends appear and are spread to the rest of the world. Of these it is important for advertising to capture the cities' people, regardless of what it is called. In big cities consumption often becomes a form of social play that spreads itself (clothing, food, fashion, music, etc). The commercial value of reaching cities is enormous and often fast globally. If you can make it in New York, you can make it anyway the saying goes, but today the same applies to all cities with populations in the millions.

Many major cities around the world such as Paris, São Paulo and even a number of US cities, have banned or greatly restricted outdoor advertising. Soon, we may see entire cities, even entire countries with such regulations. Why not build a brand town instead or a brand country? Cities such as London, New York and Dubai are already brands. Why not build towns named P&G or have a centre called Google Downtown?

"It's all about daring to try new roads..."
Stina Honkamaa, CEO, Google Sweden

For Google, these roads can lead anywhere and just as Las Vegas was built from nothing in the middle of the desert, so Google can create its own city. Critics might argue that such a city would be just another Disneyland, but a number of today's brands have more going for them than many of today's cities. With the current level of tourism, many cities actually could use Disneyland as a benchmark. Many companies produce more income than entire countries.

The step to building a city isn't as big as it seems. Companies such as Nokia already use neighbouring regions to test new concepts such as new payment systems using mobile phones. Just think if they could build an entire city where we could test the future today – fans, employees and creative talents, all giving energy to the brand tribe. So who would be interested? Just look at all the conventions where fans get together. Give them a town and they'll run it on pure enthusiasm! Instead of conventional outdoor advertising, the inhabitants would live the brand and develop it from the inside to spread it around the world.

> *The first stage could be branded buildings built as brand icons – for example, an iPod skyscraper. The next step is attracting people to the town. Would you live in a brand if it was rent free and full of cool people? As for cost, building a town is cheaper than many super-brands spend on advertising. Of course, it would only work with well-liked brands. Apple could easily fill an entire country with fans. On the other hand, how many hackers would move to Microsoft Town?*

Moving business forward

The reason that so many of today's companies have stood still is quite simply that they *could*. On a transparent market, however, competition is increasing and moving forward is no longer *an* option, it's the *only* option. The purpose of advertising is not to create its own reality, but rather to serve the needs and goals of its clients. By opening the door to the market and welcoming the customer's input, advertising can play a central role in a company's future.

> *Too many brands are using advertising as lipstick; instead they could use advertising to interact to integrate consumers with their brand DNA/personality.*

The purpose of this book is to help open that door and let advertising fulfil its promise by moving business forward and adding real value to consumers' lives. Current management models are antiquated and in desperate need of the fresh approaches that the advertising industry can offer. Why else would so many of today's icon brands such as Apple, IKEA and Dell depend on the vision of a single person instead of relying on the company DNA? (We will return to this theme in *An Elevator Pitch to Top Management.*)

Based on innovation and not the traditional case race

I tend to read too many business books and find myself drowning in all the cases. In order for this book not to become part of this *case race,* I have spent a lot of time interviewing people who are *not* in traditional business – priests (about our need for faith), behavioural psychologists, brain researchers, psychologists, one of the world's few professors of parapsychology (communication is very intuitive…), gaming companies such as Grin, chess masters, space agencies (the next step for mankind), gamers, manga fans, fans, company bloggers and consumers. Then I started interviewing CEOs and key people in advertising, media and PR agencies such as Grey, Ogilvy, Lowe, Publicis, JKL Group, Gyro, OMD, Carat and word-of-mouth agencies. I even attended PR seminars with hundreds of big names in the industry arranged by companies such as Hill & Knowlton. I talked to leaders at IT companies such as Farfar, Great Works, StarDolls and MySpace as well as CEOs at interesting organizations such as the Association of Advertisers, the Trade Federation and the Marketing Federation. And finally, I interviewed CEOs and marketing directors at GM and PR directors at companies such as Philips, all to give a more complete picture of what is necessary to move business forward. You don't have to agree 100% with my ideas, but I guarantee that you will find a spark or two of inspiration to move your business forward...and into space.

According to the 2007 report from the Institute of Practitioners in Advertising (UK):

> *"Tomorrow's consumers will be increasingly hard to reach over the next ten years so agencies will need to re-invent themselves to adapt."*
>
> ipa.co.uk

Reinventing yourself applies not only to ad agencies, but to anyone who wants to reach consumers. You'll notice that many examples in the book are from Sweden. This actually makes my book *more* relevant for the rest of the world. Sweden is often referred to as the world's R&D department, partially due to the amount of ground-breaking work that is done here, but also due to the number of companies and products that have used the country as a test market. Because of its transparency, centralized statistical infrastructure, stable democracy, high standard of living, high level of consumer awareness and manageable size, Sweden is used to test everything from new toothpaste to new pharmaceuticals.

Sweden is innovative because it simply has no choice. The domestic market is too small and the country has long been forced to turn to exports to succeed. Its dark winters foster reflection and innovations that can compete on the international market. These innovations are as Swedish as they are international. Swedish brands, for example, are often as much about a sort of cultural democracy as the country itself. IKEA is an example of a super-brand that exports Swedish democracy in the form of products. If you go even further back in history, the Vikings created a very democratic export economy. They were good at building boats and as their domestic economy was practically non-existent, their enterprising spirit carried them all over the world in search of new markets (Strid/Andréasson, 2007).

Once advertising was all about sending out a message,
like a radio antenna. Consumers nowadays have more power to
choose whether or not they wish to receive that message.

Today, it is more about taking IN a message. It's not until brands
reach IN that their values can develop a social standing in the tribe.
If the message is accepted, it is the tribe's own members that act as radio
transmitters to send the message on. It used to be the doctor who had the
difficult task of deciding who should live or die. Today it is the patient
groups that determine which medicines shall live or die on the market.

Football attracts millions of fans all over the world. How can we do the same for brands? How do we get consumers to dress in brand colours in the same way they do for football? A strong brand can become a sort of communal campfire where the tribe gathers. In our online world, a tribe can spread the word to a massive audience for a miniscule price (Balter, 2008).

> *"The first person who bought a fax machine was*
> *an idiot because there was nobody to fax to."*
>> Kevin Kelly, Ted.com

That "idiot" was motivated to spread the word and build his tribe of fax users. In fact, the value of the product depended on successfully spreading the word. Where are tomorrow's "idiots"?

Tribes are brand building

Humans are herd animals; we seek a sense of belonging. The Internet becomes our tribe's easily, both big and globally through opportunities such as Facebook and others offer. It changes the conditions for how brands communicate; the recipient is often a representative for a herd and not just an individual consumer. In a world where everyone can find each other via the Net, they can quickly become very big racial groups/tribes and they influence today's brands often more than the brands influence them. What the tribe writes about on blogs becomes more meaningful for mass media than all of the world's press releases. Mass media wants to simply talk about what people talk about on blogs, communities, patient groups and more. By reaching the tribe you also reach mass media that wants to be one with its readers. Many complain that they have lost control over communication. They're mistaken – communication is always based on a sender and a receiver – it's just that the receiver has changed. The receiver now demands more control over the message. Relevance in communication is now more about finding the right frequency for the sender and the receiver to find each other. The upside is that when the communication works, the receiver quickly turns into a communicator that relays the message on to a much larger group and with more credibility via *both* the digital and real world grapevine. Advertising agencies are beginning to see that non-commercial communication can be very powerful and are trying to reach into communities rather than just broadcasting more or louder.

> *"Tribes are the most effective media channels ever."*
> Seth Godin, *Tribes: We Need You to Lead Us*

When Amazon.com put its advertising money into offering free delivery, they in effect made the customer the main advertising medium. They understood that setting a common goal with the customer (free delivery = customer satisfaction) is the best advertising.

> *Customized advertising that works for different tribes*
> *will grow, today thousands of communities/tribes are*
> *started online every day and they all have unique*
> *demands (or want to feel unique).*

Communicating a particular message requires a receptive tribe with the right mix of geography and distribution. The message must be attached not only to a brand, but also a product/service that gives the customer the right experience and is in tune with the tribe's development. Malcolm Gladwell pointed this out in a speech at Ted.com (2004) where he said that quality is not about the sender, but the receiver. Quality is individual.

> *"By embracing the diversity of human beings,*
> *we will find a sure way to true happiness."*
> Malcolm Gladwell, Ted.com

This is why Procter & Gamble always puts such emphasis on the consumer at home, even though they have 9,000 employees working in its R&D department. Using input from billions of consumers, they have been able to create relevance for the development of their products and marketing. The right input is the key to giving consumers what they want.

I asked Kai Taubert, Associate Director of External Business Development at Procter & Gamble this question: Can consumers really suggest updates on products or even totally new products?

> *"Absolutely. There is a place on pg.com for consumers to submit suggestions. That, however, is completely different from Connect + Develop (C+D). C+D is about finding solutions – existing property – to meet P&G's needs. We are looking for companies or innovators with patents, trademarks, copyrights, etc – someone who 'owns' something. You can't own an idea, so if you have a great suggestion, but haven't developed it and protected your rights, there is no basis for a business transaction. We're looking for technologies, products, packaging, designs, business models and processes that have already demonstrated success and are, possibly, in the market someplace on a smaller scale."*

P&G's successful career started with visits to consumers to study how they washed and cooked. This spirit continues in the Internet age with direct contact with billions of consumers who the company can engage in a two-way dialogue via advertising and other available channels. The result is that consumers get better products and more interesting advertising as they are themselves part of the message. Big brands must find the right frequency in order to prosper or even survive in a time when the customer is king and global tribes such as Facebook, MySpace, Ning, Twitter, Meetup and eBay rule the planet. By building tribes from the inside, the brand is transformed into a mirror. When tribe members can see themselves in the brand, other consumers will also use it as a mirror.

"Without innovation, offerings become more and more like each other. They commoditize. As they do so, customers are able to play off one vendor against the next to get a lower price."

Geoffrey A. Moore, *Dealing with Darwin*

By acting interactively, big companies can muster the courage to be more unique and exciting. By going interactive, the fans can help top management deal with their all too common fears and phobias about contact with the outside world. Let the glow from tribal campfire fire up corporate whiteboards around the world and take company stock prices with them.

"People are no longer passive receivers of advertising. We have to be entertaining to reach people today."

Mark Tutssel, Global Chief Creative Officer,
Leo Burnett

Travelling and lecturing I often get the question: is it really good to ask the consumer what they want, after all they don't know what they want. Isn't it better to surprise them? This is a good question, but a bad attitude. Nowadays, you don't have the luxury of waiting until someone else asks your consumers what they want.

Today, customer dialogue is low priority and far down in the organizational hierarchy of most companies. If companies such as P&G, however, can bring these issues into top management, other companies will also be forced to listen and learn. *Passion drives business, but if no one is driving, brands will park their innovation – and that's where we are today.*

This is when advertising must reach IN rather than just OUT. As we move to an ever more segmented market, everyone theoretically talks to everyone else. The narrower the brand, the easier word of mouth spreads to other target groups. Gmail.com and Spotify.com spread like wildfire just *because* it was limited to five friends by recommendation only. Trend-sensitive industries such as music and fashion often use this sort of tactic.

Chris Andersson's book *The Long Tail*, explains how even products that appeal to only a very small group can be profitable in a digital age. It is this "long tail" that allows Amazon.com to sell highly specialized books to small groups and make a profit doing so.

The opposite of the Long Tail

Instead of starting from the high demand end of the curve and working your way down along the long tail, you can start out at the tip of the tail and follow the growth of the tribe up to a wider audience. Start by creating a unique and authentic platform from the beginning and move up from there.

There's nothing new about using stories to build tribes; native peoples have done it for thousands of years. What's news is that the business world has started to do it. Stanford professor Chip Heath and his co-author Dan Heath have examined the subject in their book *Made to Stick* by analyzing which sort of stories stick in our minds and which don't. It's all about packaging a story so that everyone who hears it will want to share it with someone else.

After talking to the legendary Chief Oren Lyons along with psychologists and brain researchers, I am more convinced than ever that stories are the key to how we organize our memories. Good stories get remembered.

> *In a world of tribes we look for leaders to lead us*
> *(not to push us around).*

All over the world, tribes are growing with help from the Internet. People find ideas, common interests and brands to connect around. According to the book *Tribes: We Need You to Lead Us* by Seth Godin, tribes will explode in numbers and become one of the biggest growth industries of our time. To prove his point, Seth Godin is now building his own tribe at Triiibes.com. In other words, today's brands need to function as a tribal meeting place in order to succeed.

From anti-advertising to a fishhook future

A number of pessimistic advertising gurus I met while writing this book have said:

> *"We are the last generation of admen!"*

Many people warned me against writing a book about something so non-trendy as advertising. Who will read it?

I haven't heard so many negative reactions since my advertising friends told me they didn't dare tell anybody in the 70s that they worked in advertising – they were at the low end of the social ladder ("Tell my mother I play piano in a brothel. If she knew I was in advertising, it would break her heart", goes an old saying.) Advertising was once trendy and will be again; trends come and go. When advertising no longer works as well as before, it's not longer just a matter of making changes in the way you work or increasing your media budget.

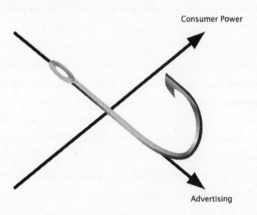

In this time of change, the advertising industry has a golden opportunity to turn the negativity towards advertising by involving consumers on *their* terms, by hooking the message on to the enormous power that consumers represent on the market.

When the consumer is king (and queen), advertising
has to make sense – now, more than ever.

Harnessing the potential of their enthusiasm and power to change requires new thinking and genuineness on today's transparent market.

Advertising as a sponsor of life

"Ads on the subway? That's so 20th century. By sponsoring the whole line
and making trips free, the local merchants' association brings grateful
commuters to neighbourhood shops" (Chris Anderson, *FREE*).

"Use free as a marketing tool to reach consumers who
can become heavy users."
Chris Anderson, *Lecture at Media Evolution (2009)*

Chris Andersson's next book, due out in 2009, is called *Free* – a key
word in the future of advertising and the big picture. When Google buys
up big companies with exciting software, which they then give to their
customers free of charge, they know very well what they're doing. It has
always seemed strange to me that for the rich and famous, most of their
consumption is sponsored – food, products, travel. Why not do this for
the people who actually made these brands successful in the first place?
Couldn't a major brand build a city where everyone lived for free? An ad
town? Many would say the very idea is absurd, but the day that someone
actually crunches the numbers, it may very well become a reality. It's just
an extension of IKEA's idea of a free bus from the city to their store. That
bus could just as well be an entire city.

"You don't value Google less because it's free.
Where you spend your time is the value."
Chris Anderson, *Lecture at Media Evolution (2009)*

Let the king and queen do more business

In my latest book *ONE – A Consumer Revolution* (Engeseth, 2006), I examine in depth the subject of consumers as kings and queens that are changing the entire face of business.

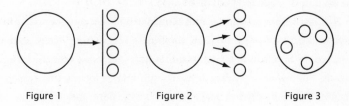

Figure 1   Figure 2   Figure 3

Mass communication (figure 1) is where the same message is broadcast to everyone. The next step takes us closer to the individual's needs (one-to-one) where every relationship is more unique (figure 2). The third mental step is to become one with the market and the customer (figure 3). In my book I go deeper and add communication and innovation to speed up business and increase competitiveness. Here is what ONE looks like taken to the next step with advertising as its motor.

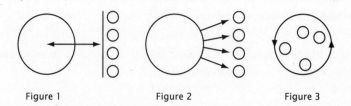

Figure 1   Figure 2   Figure 3

Making all mass communication interactive in all advertising (figure 1). One-to-one (figure 2) means having different tribes, connecting with them and learning from them. ONE is the ultimate stage of consumer interaction, but it is also the stage where the company and consumers are ONE tribe (figure 3) This stage is where the organization learns faster with interaction from the "reality" that consumers offer. But it's also where the organization learns how to take the business even further. When the border between business and consumers is moved or removed altogether, it is easier to steer the business in the same direction that the customer is moving and connect top management with the passion and innovation that fans have to offer.

If corporations such as General Motors don't listen soon, we will soon have millions of companies such as Chinese Lifan Group. Lifan started by learning how to manufacture motorcycles, cars and busses for large brands, but are now producing their own brands for the international market. If they succeed in connecting with the consumer rebellion, the established car makers will be in trouble.

Show me the money by going beyond Web 3.0

Today's advertising budgets may seem like big money, but it's all chump change compared to the money that moves at every level of the chain of consumption. Unfortunately, doing business today can often resemble working with countless islands with no connection to the mainland. This is where advertising has a role to play.

Broadening the definition of advertising will create greater resources both for others and the ad industry itself. In the digital world, you never waste half your advertising budget.

> *"Life today is digital."*
>
> Alan Rosenfeld, Business
> Development Manager, Apple

Never run over a dog or a consumer

Man's best friend is a wolf that has been bred to become a loyal companion. Most brands, unfortunately, are still bloodthirsty wolves hounding consumers with rabid advertising. The original cover of *The Fall of Adver-*

tising & the Rise of PR was a dog that had been run over (the brand symbol for Pets.com). Today's advertising needs more brands that can avoid getting run over by the bloody realities of doing business.

> *Today the dog is waving its Long Tail towards*
> *the possibilities advertising offers.*

As a kid, my family had a St. Bernard dog. This sort of dog has a long history of saving people in snowstorms. Wherever we went, our dog would always find its way back home. Good advertising always finds its way back to the client's bottom line.

Sometimes it's the advertising that helps save the dog. This is what happened at TBWA advertising with its campaign for Pedigree aimed at saving homeless dogs. The agency helped set up a store on Times Square in New York where people could adopt dogs and a site where these people could share their pet adoption stories (Dogsrule.com).

The upside for the client Pedigree was that the new pet owners would probably buy their dog food products.

But why stop there? When Sony developed their robot dog they proved just how strong the demand for a pet was. Imagine if Pedigree could take its idea one step further by making the decision to buy a dog a little easier: by offering a dog-sharing plan where Pedigree actually owned the dog and you just bought food. Or, perhaps, more down to earth would be to expand the role of the dog as a scientifically proven treatment for everything from depression to arthritis. The market for dogs with specific abilities will probably expand beyond just seeing-eye dogs for the blind. As the concept of dog ownership changes, there may well be a market for "summer dogs" or "rent-a-dog" to give both the future dog owner and the homeless dog a better chance of finding each other. As for the branding – there's no need to actually name the dogs Pedigree, but word of mouth will make the connection obvious and profitable for everyone.

Consumer revolution changed the rules

In my last book *ONE – A Consumer Revolution for Business* I wrote: "The gap between consumers and corporations is as wide as the Grand Canyon, full of missed opportunities just waiting to be converted into big business." Corporations are starting to understand the opportunities in this Grand Canyon; it's hard to miss the success stories of P&G, eBay, YouTube, Google and other brands that have made their fortunes on just this gap. These brands were not created from a distance by remote control, but by inviting consumers into the brand. Thanks to the consumer revolution focus of the my book *ONE*, I had the honour of speaking at the same seminar as Chris Andersson who wrote the mega-bestseller *The Long Tail;* a book that has forced many companies to turn their whiteboards upside down. Consumer power means big business for those who can tap into it. This, of course, changes the rules of advertising. Today's brands are swimming against the stream when they try to build brands with old-school control…sorry, management. The costs exceed the results, which leads to a panic-stricken chase after consumers instead of taking time to tune into new brand frequencies.

Consumer power is like a pair of swim fins – it can either help you move forward or it can trip you up. A message that's based on what's important to the receiver can give a brand incredible power. Who would say no to millions of hits on YouTube?

Freedom of choice – a new dimension

Getting employees to go the extra few inches can make the difference between success or failure. The problem is that free choice can't be bought. The difference between heart and salary is becoming more and more noticeable on the company's bottom line.

> *"Free will disappear if the Swedish Church is turned into a brand."*
>
> Ewa Lindqvist Hotz, Minister in the Church of Sweden

Corporate cultures such as IKEA have often been compared to religions. When the company recently needed 1,000 new managers, 50% of the applications came from people already employed at the company. The idea was to hire those who had already given their hearts to the brand. The result was a triumph of free choice (Lindquist, 2007).

The half billion dollar concern RNB Retail and Brands understands this connection and included an appropriate chapter in its annual report for 2006/2007 entitled "Love Project". This emotional message is considered a vital branding component. The attitude of employees is an essential part of integrating the brand with consumers. Say that only 1 of 10 consumers who walk into a store buys something. That figure can easily go up to 2 of 10 with the right atmosphere. Customers who feel that they are understood buy more and spend more (Solberg, 2008). Love is profitable. Mikael Solberg, CEO and President of RNB, used one of the company's sales people, Ingeborg Authried at NK (a premium department store in Stockholm) as a classic example of "free choice". By being a bit more personal and giving that little bit extra, Ingeborg Authried has attracted regular customers from all over the world (Authried, 2008). When one person can spread so much energy, what can't an entire company accomplish? For RNB, it may well mean an extra hundred million in next year's annual report.

The moment of truth is when the consumer decides to buy. If employees don't have what it takes to deliver, there is no amount of marketing in the world that can save the sale.

"Our hotels are our most important media channel."
Riitta Östberg, Marketing Manager,
Choice Hotels, Sweden

A smile costs nothing, but can be the difference between staying or going to the next hotel. Hotels are as Riitta Östberg points out – the main media channel where all success starts. Remember: *change comes from choice.*

This book is built on points not pages

That's the reason you won't find 300 pages in the book. The book will not follow a logical progression from A to Z for the simple reason that future of business won't either. Nor will it give you a finished blueprint. Instead it will be more of a signpost towards a more profitable future for consumers, advertising agencies and their clients.

Al and Laura's book is a milestone and the observations in this book are only to meant to mark the miles that we have travelled since the book was written. It has never been my ambition to write a sequel.

It is not necessary to read their book before you read this book (although I recommend it). Al Ries has in many ways created the business we call branding. The Ries book points out that advertising uses more animals than you can find at your local zoo.

Since then, the number of species has been reduced significantly.

Time to re-think the use of animals in advertising. True, as I mentioned earlier, it is easier to get something into the mind of the consumer if it can attach to something that is already there. The problem is that we're now living on a planet where many animals are endangered. Consumers' increasing green consciousness is making its mark on the world of advertising. For the time being, animals continue to populate advertising in large numbers, but what about the future? Can you expect an animal to visit you in your hotel? Well, yes...maybe.

In Singapore, I awoke to bird song in my hotel room; there were real birds in the lobby atrium.

Saving the planet can give new life to animals in advertising.
Fake commitment is very quickly ousted on the Web. Here, though,
it's the real McCoy in an ad from Choice Hotels' in-house agency.

As consumers' environmental concern increases, perhaps the borders between hotel and farm will start to blur. Take the case of Dreamfarm.

> *"Dreamfarm is our dream project. We dream about living and*
> *being involved in the countryside and are convinced that there*
> *are many others who feel the same way, but don't have the time*
> *to take care of a farm or the resources to buy a country home.*
> *To solve this problem, we plan to build a farm together with*
> *consumers, farmers and entrepreneurs so that we can combine our*
> *dream of being involved in the countryside and having a country*
> *home with the opportunity to contribute to a better environment."*

> Peopleowned.org

When I met the founder of Dreamfarm, John Higson, he said: "You never
create any change without involvement." Both survival and success are
about creating involvement.

Fakes don't build brands, fans or tribes

As a consultant, I am often invited to meetings where the CEO says: "I read your book *ONE* about how to be ONE with consumers. Can you tell me how we can sound like we're doing all this consumer revolution stuff?" The fake is alive and well, but not for long.

> *"When chickens are full of steroids, and tomatoes are*
> *engineered for transportation logistics, it's no wonder*
> *things can feel fake. Only companies that are prepared*
> *to 'walk the talk' can become real."*
>
> Higson, 2007

According to the PR industry, practically all information about health-related products is placed by PR agencies or directly by corporate communications departments. It's gone so far that there are actually price lists of celebrities and their illnesses that PR agencies "sell" to pharmaceutical companies. The lists are often used to introduce new pharmaceuticals and celebrities make good copy. So when a patient has read such and such an article and asks his doctor about the new preparation, it is often the result of pure marketing.

Nowadays, the Internet acts as a sort of counterweight to this sort of slanted information. Many fakes have been tracked down to a specific PR agency by bloggers causing enormous damage to the agency, the brand and the company behind it. Fakes, lies and greenwash can mean big money, but also big risks of getting caught.

In our digital age, there is a growing market for companies that can fill the gap between companies and consumers with real content. A case in point is the Stockholm advertising agency Farfar's campaign for Diesel Jeans that created consumer interest via a simple campaign site. The campaign placed a number of supermodels such as Heidi Klum in a hotel room with Web cams piping advertising videos directly to the site. Naturally, the films were popular items on YouTube and the campaign succeeded in giving the advertising a dimension of pull.

When I interviewed Farfar CEO, Matias Palm-Jensen, I understood why the agency is world-class. The Diesel campaign attracted fans and also created a new brand "Heidies", a tribute to both the Diesel brand and Heidi Klum. Unfortunately, Diesel didn't see the entire potential. They missed a chance to feed their brand.

An amusing side-effect of the Diesel campaign is that a certain demand has now been created for a brand call Heidi. The question remains if Heidi herself will take the opportunity to develop this brand.

Mattias Palm-Jensen tells how his agency *creates* time instead of *buying* time for advertising. In some cases, it's a matter of creating entertainment. In other cases it's about opening channels for consumers to participate. When we met, the agency had just gotten a request from Reebok about how to create time by adding personality and colour to their brand.

> *"We don't want to be a radio channel for Reebok;*
> *we want to be the radio."*
>
> Matias Palm-Jensen, CEO, Farfar

It will be interesting to see how the battle with Adidas plays out and if Reebok manages to take market share. Mattias expresses it succinctly.

> *"Bad advertising is just another way of saying here,*
> *come and take our market."*

If brands don't listen and learn, they can't work with free thinkers such as Mattias or with smart consumers. This is why so many brands today are looking for stupid consumers.

Real vs. fake

In the thought-provoking and funny film *Crazy People* (1990) an ad-man (Dudley Moore) is sent to a mental hospital where he does the only logical thing: he starts an ad agency. He and the other patients turn out advertising that simply tells the truth and creates great advertising. Volvos "They're boxy, but they're good"; Cigarettes: "Lung cancer? Perhaps. Flavour? For sure!"; United Airlines: "Most of our passengers get there alive."

Funny, but true

In 2008, McDonald's is trying to counter bad press with its "I'm lovin' it!" campaign. The result has been a wealth of YouTube parodies and falling sales figures (a broken mirror). Wouldn't it be better if they could be inspired by Dudley Moore's character and find a more genuine, more honest way of communicating? Large companies often equate successful advertising with big agency million dollar viral film campaigns designed to look home-made. Companies such as Brandname.com offer product placement in amateur films on YouTube helping brands to fake consumer involvement. The backlash is hate-websites, as well as short and even full-length films exposing the bluffs. One documentary that should be every company's worst nightmare is the anything-but-flattering *Wal-Mart: The High Cost of Low Price* (2005), showing how entire regions are fighting the spread of Wal-Mart (Walmartmovie.com). Instead of building towns, Wal-Mart is getting anti-brand-towns.

"If you want to be cynical – but realistic – the definition of marketing could be: marketing is a set of tricks to squeeze maximum, short-term profits out of consumers, citizens, other companies and the government, to the benefit of the management and shareholders of the supplier."

Professor Evert Gummesson,
Total Relationship Marketing

It's time to face the fact that faking it can cost more money in the long run than doing the right thing to begin with. Many consumers are realizing that the reason so many companies are faking it is that their products and services don't hold up in the light of day.

This is where advertising has a role to play by bringing the customer closer to the company to create an offering that is worthy to be called a modern brand. The fake factor is not about advertising, but rather about the company behind it. Far too many of today's large companies are built on fake brands. This fakeness is often the result of the distance between management decisions and the real world. Making cars and cigarettes is easy; sitting in a car when it crashes or holding the hand of a dying smoker is not (Gummesson, 2008). The transparent market makes it possible for both sender and receiver to see each other. This is the beginning of mutual respect. In the old days when the chef walked around in the restaurant to talk with the guests, he would not only get feedback on the food, but also develop a face-to-face relationship with his "fans".

Today's management has the tools to reach out to its customers and create participation and integrity on sites such as Linkedin.com, MySpace.com, Flickr.com and Bebo.com as well as communities such as Twitter.com, Jaiku.com and Socialthing.com. Yet even here, the age-old impulse to fake it can shine through. Why not approach it honestly by letting the company or ad agency participate without trying to sell anything. Let it listen and learn like the rest of us. A great place to begin is Blogcatalog.com, a site that makes it possible to gather all your online relationships in one place. It's easier to keep up with trends by reading one page than reading 100's of blogs using RSS or a news reader such as Newsgator.com. Remember the old adage that you only exist in relation to other people.

> *"The reason children are so good at adapting to new technology is that they don't have a choice. They're adapting to their future."*
>
> Per Hamid Ghatan, Brain Researcher,
> Karolinska Institutet

Perhaps this is how advertising should adapt to the new dimensions that social networking media offer (the learning process is step-by-step.) Only then can these newfound social skills be applied to the brand. Brands such as Audi (tv.audi.com) and Tommy Hilfiger (tommytv.com) started by building social platforms first. It's important to see this kind of branding as a long-term commitment and not just a campaign or a monologue. When brands create their own media channels they become less dependent on big name media (Coke and Ford can now use each other's channels.) If they are successful, they can build companies and save brands in hard times. Loyal fans have saved many companies from bankruptcy (However, if fans commit time and energy and are disappointed, fans will become anti-fans who turn viciously on the brand.)

When Saab introduced a classic Saab Turbo in a limited black edition, fans quickly blogged it as "the black turbo is back" and posted animations such as a short about a Saab and Darth Vader. Fans can often go so much further than companies because they can create a more genuine tone and have freer hand in stretching intellectual property rights. Saab supports the fans with information, but no content. The result is that the brand gets millions of visitors on platforms that cannot be bought for any amount of money. Cars, just like communities, are built on platforms (Ries, 2008). At the time of this writing in 2009, it looks like Darth Vader here has moved the Saab brand into darker parts of the brand parking space. If they would use more input from their fan tribe they would sell more cars than they could produce. When a brand has got lost, it is often good to go back to its origins. I suggested that they produce the first car they ever made, the so-called "ur-Saab", model 92001. According to my taste one of the most beautiful cars ever made, and unlike today's SAAB cars, it is completely unique. If they made it in a retro version environmentally-friendly motors and technology, it would easily fit in my garage, and most likely in those of the entire fan tribe that would then get something unique to unify itself around. Then the new customers can build fan tribes around the relationship, as between them in relation to the unique "Ur Saab". It is the degree of uniqueness that determines how truly a brand is experienced.

PART ONE

The Fall of PR

10 points that are speeding up the fall of PR

1. PR can no longer fly under the nonsense (or BS) radar. Today's smart consumers see through PR messages in the media.

2. PR agencies can no longer hide the truth. With 100 million bloggers, media is no longer "the third party", but rather, just one of many voices.

3. The PR industry is doing very little for their clients' brand strategy and clients are starting to catch on.

4. A parrot can learn to say *branding* and *advertising*, but that doesn't necessarily mean he understands what they mean. (Feel free to substitute *executive* for *parrot*...)

5. Greed and competition have driven PR agencies to sell press clippings by the kilo. The result: PR has become easier to spot as artificially generated and not an especially good bargain.

6. PR agencies love crisis management – not for the challenge, but for the money. Crisis management is a cash cow and is often sold by the same agency doing the rest of the PR.

7. With limited online savvy, PR agencies' attempts to fake their way into reputable forums often backfire. (Several agencies have already been ousted for fake postings.)

8. PR agencies are nowhere near delivering what their customers are asking for. Nine out of ten of their customers surveyed aren't sure what they're paying for.

9. A lack of rules and ethics often drives PR agencies to go too far. (Or maybe selling seriously ill celebrities as spokespersons for pharmaceutical company products is OK? It seems that reality is more Sicko than Michael Moore's film...)

10. Due to time restraints and competition from the Web, much of what passes for news has no credible source. Try it yourself: check the sources in the newspapers you read this week. If you can find one article with a real source, one without a profit motive, frame that article. It may be the last one of its kind.

Greed killed PR's credibility

The main factor for successful PR is the objectivity of the "third party", an objectivity that has often been exposed as anything but thanks to smart consumers. Ironically, it is the increasing success and visibility of PR that is the greatest threat to its future.

> *"Traditional media have lost in power through websites and blogs that are controlled by citizens who can get messages through at little cost without being censored or edited by anyone else."*
> Professor Evert Gummesson, *Total Relationship Marketing*

Competition from digital media has meant that journalists have much shorter deadlines and smaller budgets. This has opened the way for PR consultants to deliver finished material such as articles and studies. I've interviewed a number of eminent PR consultants who have told me that the media climate makes it much easier to plant "news"– that is, PR. To get noticed in all the media static, you have to be provocative, which is often a synonym for stretching the truth. There's no bigger difference between selling cars or selling stories to the media. The same consultant agrees consumers are getting much better at telling news from PR, using his own children as examples. That generation goes to Google and looks at the facts and then spreads its own version of the information to friends on Facebook. It's a kind of inverted *Tipping Point* (Gladwell, 2002). Researchers have seen indications that young consumers are getting much better at seeing through PR (Dahlen, 2008).

Malcolm Gladwell's book, *Blink* (2007), shows how a few seconds is often more than enough to get a feel for if something is real or fake. If we can spot a fake *Mona Lisa*, seeing through fake PR is no problem. All it takes is one person to blow the whistle and overnight the message is on millions of blogs. A sign of the times is that many large companies are now changing *Press* in their menus to *Press & Bloggers*.

One example is Wecansolveit.org, a grassroots organization that reaches over 1.9 million people. They encourage bloggers to register for news that can reach a global audience. Naturally, this approach also gives journalists a new channel to reach people they normally couldn't because of conflicts of interest with the large corporations that own many of the media channels. Barack Obama would never have had a chance of becoming the President if it hadn't been for the digital grassroots movement of 2 million volunteers spreading the message across the country. Obama now has a wonderful opportunity to use this tribe of two million strong to participate in creating a new USA. Name a brand, city, country or president that can succeed without the power of the volunteer or enthusiast? There is no London or Washington without their inhabitants (take a look at London.gov.uk/onelondon – a platform where 7 million London inhabitants can share photographs and stories about their great city.) Make a note: the time of monologues is over.

Even the lie is a lie in PR…

PR is also used in today's smear campaigns or to ruin a competing brand in order to replace it with something else. This is called *black PR*. Some PR agencies work with both sides because, unlike advertising, which agency is doing what for which client is not public knowledge. It may sound like a bad joke, but it has actually happened: competitors have run into each other at PR agency parties.

> *"Commercial PR must become more openly commercial.*
> *Being straight about what you stand for creates tolerance.*
> *What's hidden becomes false. In the media static we're*
> *searching for the genuine."*
>
> Robert Bryhn, CEO, Ogilvy Advertising, Sweden

Parrots can only imitate brand building

I once had a parrot. I remember I used to give it nuts to teach it to talk. We started with small words and gradually moved up to longer phrases.

I even taught it to say the magical words "brand building". PR people learned to talk about branding when people started giving them nuts called "marketing budgets". Some may have learned a little too fast for their own good, even faster than my parrot. There is a fine line between learning by imitation and understanding. Many PR agencies can imitate branding, but brands such as Dell, Google, Starbucks, Zara, H&M and Harley-Davidson, were not created in a PR agency. They were created by business people who knew how to create consumer satisfaction.

Overkill PR for
Thai Air

Giving reporters discounts on airline tickets is not always a good idea. Thai Air is a classic case of how to damage a brand with PR overkill. This is how the company's PR person explained it: "We're not interested in having reporters write about Thailand! We only want them to write about Thai Air…" (Resume.se, 2007). Wow, is there really a brand called Thai Air that is completely separate from Thailand? I don't think so. Compare this with Singapore Airlines. This airline has taken the exact opposite approach and has made Singapore an integral part of the brand; a brand, by the way, that is flying quite high at the moment.

PR pimped BBC
for the devil

Al Gore's film marked a change in direction in public opinion on global warming, a change that frightened many in the corporate world. One response was a barrage of PR in the media trying to create doubt on a fairly straight-forward issue. A surprising number of media articles where dismissed as pure PR marketing. Even the respected institution the BBC was taken in and aired a documentary that amounted to a corporate commercial entitled *The Great Global Warming Swindle*. Within a matter of hours the film had been panned by a firestorm of millions of bloggers around the world. The film was dismissed as PR and its credibility torn apart.

PR is too slow for today's business world

The classic brand building formula in the Ries book of building the brand gradually over time, then supporting it with advertising, no longer applies. Today's PR agencies are starting ad agencies to be able to offer their clients a single "big bang". It's quite simply an economic calculation. As R&D and product cycles get shorter and competition gets tougher, many don't have the time to build slowly. It is vital to build a brand before the product is copied. Making a profit means taking market share as quickly as possible. The old saying: *Here today, gone tomorrow* also goes for PR.

PR agencies can't even spell the Internet

Of course, you really can't blame PR agencies for doing their job, only that they often do it so badly. When the company is exposed in the transparent world of the Web, they call their PR agency for crisis management for the crisis they themselves helped to create. Bloggers often have more technical and media savvy than most agencies, which means that efforts by PR agencies to blend in on the Web are about as graceful as an elephant in a tutu. What's worse, bloggers are more and more on their guard against intruders using word of mouth, passwords or by restricting access through scalable communities where there are different levels of access for getting or leaving information.

PR's porno reality

The porno business has developed a standard sex format that's fake through and through. It has nothing to do with reality and is full of silicone implants and bad acting. In a lot of ways, PR is providing the media with a sort of porno reality. That's why I have been known to call it "PR - Porno Relations". Much of what passes for real news is just marketing. Then, along came Web 2.0 and the game started to change. Consumers themselves started defining reality for themselves on sites ranging from Wikipedia to YouTube. They even took over actual pornography with sites such as YouPorn.com where all content is provided by the users themselves.

Why bad client results make money for PR agencies

Strangely enough, when things go badly for the client, PR agencies actually make more money. Crisis management is worth much more in billed hours than daily PR work. This is also the reason that PR agencies don't put a high priority on market communications training. There are simply other more profitable areas higher up on the corporate ladder.

Bank robbers, hangmen and PR people

Bank robbers and hangmen wear masks not only because of their "privacy policy" (not being identified), but also to create the emotional distance that makes their jobs easier. It's easier to do your job if you avoid building a relationship with the person you're trying to rob or execute. This depersonalization has been good for the PR industry, but not for much longer. If the industry is to prosper when its masks are pulled off, it must be in a new era of integrity where PR is sent out as such.

PR is not all bad

The PR industry is having PR problems. They've lost their anonymity, but all is not lost. To those PR people who feel offended or demonized, I have some good news for you later in the book. The fact is that daily life doesn't have enough "content" to satisfy today's demand. Here is where honest PR has a vital role to play. Advertising can and will fill much of the demand for entertaining content. What we often forget is that even the media is made up of companies that are feeling the competition from digital media. Stina Dabrowski, a prominent Swedish journalist and television personality, sums up the face of digital competition: "The biggest sports news story isn't the biggest sports news story anymore, but rather the story that was covered on that particular channel" (dn.se, 2008).

Bloggers quote the news, the news quotes the bloggers. New models and a new order will develop, but in the meantime we are left with a chaotic transition that will create openings for both media and advertisers.

PART TWO

The Rise of Advertising

10 Points that are speeding up the rise of advertising

1. The Internet is starving for content; advertising no longer needs to buy expensive media to reach its target.

2. The more advertising costs, the better it sells. However, the reverse is true for PR: the more you spend, the more likely the consumer is to react negatively.

3. The advertising agency creates the strategy for the brand and works directly with top management. The PR agency doesn't.

4. New insights into the human mind and the mechanics of tribes are easier to apply to advertising than PR. PR is a one night stand in a world where people are looking for lasting relationships with their brands.

5. Old school push advertising is being replaced by pull – good advertising is becoming as important as the brand itself.

6. When the sender of the message is clear, it is easier to reach today's smart consumers with advertising. This makes it easier for companies to develop the next iPhone, Google or Harley-Davidson.

7. The advertising industry has a solid framework and its long history is full of lessons learned.

8. In our digital world, advertising reaches more consumers faster than ever.

9. Advertising has become part of the entertainment industry. Consumers are getting more sophisticated. Well-conceived, honest ads can have impact like never before.

10. There's an old saying that half of all advertising is wasted, but we don't know which half. Today, half the value of advertising is getting smart consumers to spread the word, extending the reach of the advertising into niche groups.

Just as it is getting harder to lie in PR, it is also getting harder for companies to hide the fact that they are offering products and services that just aren't good enough. Once marketing was one large megaphone that spoke to the masses; now everyone has a megaphone and is eager to use it. It is now harder for bigger companies to stifle smaller ones. Moving fast is taking on increasing importance in the world of innovation. Business is evolving and it's time to take that evolution to advertising. It's time to make the customer's participation and enthusiasm part of the picture because these things have become more valuable than the customer's money. Reaching into consumer tribes is for many brands the only way of making an impact. Inspired consumers can create, move and develop brands that will generate consumption. The key is interaction and respect from the sender of the message, a new development in marketing.

> *"Buying a good megaphone is a lot harder than it used to be..."*
>
> Micael Dahlén, Professor, Centre for Consumer Marketing, Stockholm School of Economics

Now that traditional advertising channels to consumers are being closed and media time has become so expensive, traditional ways of working are no longer economically viable for many brands. This has opened the way for the PR industry to offer inexpensive media exposure. As the PR becomes easier to spot, however, the offer becomes less attractive. For the first time in history, the lie has become more expensive than the truth.

In these times of social media such as Facebook, advertising must change with the times. Advertising can become successful if it becomes more interactive and creates a relationship with the consumer. The industry that, in many ways, is leading the way is pharmaceuticals. Due to advertising restrictions, pharmaceutical companies have been among the first to seek direct contact with their customers. Companies such as Pfizer are looking at how to create their own social media such as Facebook.

> *"When paid advertising is prohibited, social media become the only channel straight to the consumer. This is how Pfizer reasons..."*
>
> Internetworld, 2008.

But, wouldn't it have been better to find a direct channel of communication with the customer before the conventional channels were closed off? No, because it was not dictated by the competition until increased pharmaceutical copying began forcing the industry to get closer to the patient. The relationship with the patient will also be affected by future regulation. The prognosis for the advertising industry does not look good:

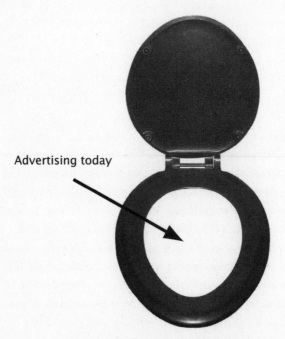

Advertising today

This could just as well have been about PR. Today's toilets know more about consumers than today's advertising.

Brands were created to protect originality. Today, it's the other way around: brands are often used to hide the original's low quality. Producing the actual product is no longer especially difficult; many brands even produce their own low-priced copies to cope with pirating. The consumer gets the exact same product for two different prices in the same retail outlet. Many companies are seeing that the original creates a demand for cheap copies that often strengthens the original brand. The bottom line is that changing advertising is not just about new tricks. It's time to involve the consumer instead of hounding him. The history of advertising reflects the history of business; the future of advertising is to *create* the future of business. Advertising will not ask the question, "Which came first, the chicken or the egg?" It will fertilize the egg while marketing it!

> *"Advertising no longer works as cosmetics. You can no longer disguise a product…"*
>
> Pia Grahn Brikell, President, Advertising Association of Sweden

One reason that advertising has had a tendency to exaggerate is that the service or product doesn't have anything unique to offer. The challenge is then to build a brand. So far, so good. Yet, good advertising cannot improve a bad offer, nor does it do anything to motivate company management. Often, people are more enthusiastic about buying the advertising than they are about buying the product.

> *"Only a campaign that makes a genuine human connection with the audience can invite the consumer to participate in your message."*
>
> Pat Fallon & Fred Senn, *Juicing the Orange*

The customer must see himself in your message; after all, who buys a mirror that you can't see yourself in? Much of my research shows that companies who make mistakes, but then learn from their customers, often create much stronger relationships with them than they would have if they had done everything right from the beginning. This has been the case with both Apple and IKEA, who made many mistakes and have learned from them. Who hasn't? But the ones who learn from it grow into big corporations. This interaction with customers rejuvenates the brand and helps consumers see themselves in it, creating real fans. Some of the worst products in history have the most enthusiastic fans. Rumour has it that motorcycle gangs were formed because the Harley-Davidson motorcycles they rode were of such terrible quality that wherever you went, you needed a friend and lots of spare parts. Classic English sports cars have a similar following. And even if a Japanese car or motorcycle costs half as much and are twice as dependable – who needs a vehicle that doesn't need you? How many people would have pets if they knew the pets didn't need them? In romantic relationships it's often the vulnerability that forms the basis for strong emotions. So why don't more brands show their vulnerability?

Harley-Davidson, Apple, IKEA – they've all shown that the advertising of the future must affect the sender as much as the receiver.

> *"Blogs, forums and communities allow us to benefit from the views of millions of others. People form opinions not by watching TV, but by discussing issues. They should discuss your brand and be free to play with it… to 'own' it by creating their own interpretation of it and to be associated with it in a "personal" way. That's where brand equity will be established."*
>
> Indiatimes.com

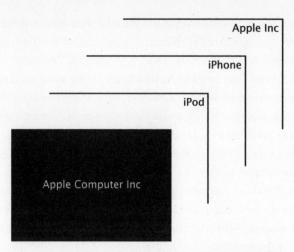

Out of the box in business life is about making the box
bigger growing the market. Apple Computer Inc. moved their
business from computers into new markets with iTunes, iPod,
iPhones, television and media. Today, they are a company with
a bigger market position than just computers and have
even renamed themselves Apple Inc.

Over the years, Apple has done a lot of cool advertising, but with modern
interactive communication in all media channels they could have learned
faster and moved from computers to today's successes in less than half the
time. By letting the "brand box" grow together with consumers and top
management, Apple has begun to let passionate fans into the company
as can be witnessed by the company's decision to let developers develop
programs for the iPhone. The company should use this approach to their
advertising as well – let the fans into the company. The choice is between
having the customer working for the company or against it.

Naturally, the best situation is when company and customer *both work
together.* The advantage is not just a more pleasant working atmosphere,
but more money budgeted for advertising as advertising has been proven
to be *essential* to the success of the business. Money rules the game of
advertising, but only if it's played well.

The game industry is thriving and has long since passed the movie business in sales. Production budgets can be bigger than for a Hollywood production and there are game companies that even have their own TV stations. The game industry has long been open for development help from consumers who contribute their modifications or mods. The hit game Counter-strike, actually started out as a mod for Half-life (Hjelmtorp, 2008). The same thing could apply to advertising, that is, letting the consumer develop new variations that are released virally, sometimes creating more of an impact than the original. Forget your ego and let in the customer. Even if you don't let the customer in, chances are he will still post something on YouTube. The difference is that by working with the consumer, chances are greater that you'll create a new best-seller.

Putting the Nobel Prize in your iPhone

The Nobel Prize is one of the strongest brands in the world. But until 2008, they haven't seen themselves as a brand. Now they've hired their first ever Marketing and Communications Manager, Merci Olsson, Nobelprize.org. I've known Merci for many years, so when we met we felt comfortable in stretching the brand to exaggerated lengths.

So, what are the limits for a brand? In the case of the Nobel Prize, if you lose control of how the brand is used, it risks losing its significance. This is where Merci comes into the picture to help her colleagues make the brand and its history more visible. Up until now the brand has been used by many different groups without any sort of quality control. In my opinion, the prize has been too "high class" to stoop to considering itself a brand and has paid the price that comes with this sort of hubris. Even if the brand is an invaluable human asset, it also has a concrete commercial value that must both be cared for and capitalized upon. So how do you use the brand and develop its meaning? One way is to spotlight the technology that the prizes have honoured. One of the prizes in physics, for example, was given to scientists that developed the technology that made ultra-small hard discs possible – iPods and other MP3 players, for example. So why not use the same technology that you have rewarded to spread the message to the world? There's no shortage of university lecture material on iTunes; why not add Nobel Prize winners and their work? This would strengthen the brand and its reach and inspire future prize-winners. Or, it might perhaps motivate young people to pursue higher studies by working with high profile media. How about using MTV to challenge teenagers to find solutions to global warming? A great way to increase interest in the sciences would be to build programs around the prizewinners, something the major universities would surely be interested in along with companies such as Apple. The grassroots appeal of a Podcast can both extend the appeal of the brand and create genuine connections that can release the enormous power that is generated when ignorance or apathy is suddenly transformed into the thirst for knowledge.

Going from intangible to tangible values means finding a balance between historical tradition and credibility on the one hand and getting the most out of a commercial brand worth billions on the other.

> *"It's all how far you have the courage to go in blurring the borders between commercial and non-commercial."*
>
> Merci Olsson, Marketing and Communications
> Manager, Nobelprize.org

Merci explained that she plans to focus more on the people behind the prizewinners, who they are, why they chose the path they did and what drives them on through long hours in the lab. Times are changing – the boundaries between institutions and the commercial world are more diffuse. More and more, we will see companies such as YouTube and Google blur the distinctions between media and learning, something that the Nobel Prize can be part of. The connection is quite natural: Google is already a sort of university. Perhaps the bonds between Google and the Nobel Prize could be strengthened through some sort of filtered search for scientific information.

Working with a brand name that causes the phones to ring all day long, is a privilege. Of course, few brands have a history that dates back to 1901. To keep the brand up to date, you could use Google Earth and let the Global Positioning System (GPS), alert your iPhone when you pass by the house of a historical prize winner. Naturally, the information would be linked to nobelprize.org and nearby libraries and bookstores where you can learn more. What makes this kind of connection so valuable is that it is so unique. This uniqueness creates word of mouth about the prize and adds a personal human element to the history behind it. Just as there is a U2 special edition of the iPod, there could be a Nobel Prize iPod. I think it's just a matter of time.

There are endless opportunities; everyone wants to bask in the credibility that shines from the Nobel Prize – magazines, newspapers, films, even TV series. By opening up to cooperation with more commercial media such as CNN, BBC and The New York Times, the Nobel Prize organization can both increase their control over their brand while creating mutually beneficial sponsoring arrangements with influential IT companies such as Honeywell or top pharmaceutical companies that can have an interest in being associated with the prize. This is an excellent example of how advertising and PR can work together.

Or in the words of Merci at the end of our interview; "It's like working in a candy shop – there's just so much chocolate here."

> *If Apple wanted to become an educational institution, it could achieve it with the ease of switching playlists on an iPod. Just think how much of the PC market would shift if Apple became a university. Not just any university, though. With mobile phones, computers and iTunes, Apple University wouldn't even need a physical campus; it would be located everywhere. They could even franchise the idea to Harvard, Princeton or Stanford. What's more, becoming a university could give them better access to the talent that will create the Googles and Nobel Prizes of tomorrow.*

Fun pays?

You've probably known it for quite some time now, but now it's confirmed by empirical research: creative companies have more fun and have happier employees (Rasulzada, 2007). Maybe it's just more fun to work at Google than at Microsoft. Both companies are highly productive and profitable, but Google has a corporate climate that attracts talent in a way Microsoft does not. Google has even been known to use gratuitous humour in its recruitment ads.

How much fun is *your* working day? Your answer to this question has a lot more to do with productivity than your financial department might think. Many of us have suspected it: employees who have fun at work are more productive. I call it "fun pays".

Fun is a double-edged sword as Metro Newspapers board member Hans-Holger Albrecht demonstrated in a speech in 2003. In a joking tone, he began his speech to a group of the company's international managers with "Good evening, ladies, gentlemen and niggers…" (Wahlberg, 2005). The incident naturally made headlines around the world, especially in the US, forcing him to resign from the board. Yet, he kept his position as CEO of the group's media group, Modern Times Group (MTG). On the one hand a company cannot afford to be associated with racism (even though this was probably not the intent of his speech). On the other hand, psychologists put great value on a sense of perspective and sense of humour for mental health and for the health of a corporate culture. In a later speech in 2008, Hans-Holger said:

> *"We don't take business too seriously."*
> Hans-Holger Albrecht, CEO, MTG

As for the health of MTG – it not only owns the world's largest free newspaper *Metro*, but also a portfolio of media holdings in radio, online, TV and satellite (Viasat). Sales for 2007 passed €1 billion.

Fun pays in world records – gold, silver and bronze.

The Olympic Games in Beijing 2008 produced a number of examples of *fun pays*. The men's 100 metres, for example, was won by a smiling and dancing Jamaican who also set a world record. Jamaica's women were just as laid back when they won gold, silver and bronze. They all laughed themselves to victory. Who knows, maybe a smile is the best antidote to fear of failure. "Laughing all the way to the bank" may be true both as a saying and as a term for corporate culture. It all sounds so simple, yet there are so many companies that have invested in solutions that are a mystery to everyone at the company. When employees are one with the brand, the company comes out a winner. Being part of the equation and the winning team creates meaning and motivation. Problems and challenges that seem insurmountable for the individual, can be solved together, turning vision into results.

This is how Southwest Airlines changed the entire airline industry while increasing the value of their stock by hundreds of percent.

Playing it safe was never what the company's CEO Herb Kelleher had in mind. Or as they put it in the legendary book Nuts! about Southwest Airlines.

> "The company realized early on that the more outrageous
> it was, the more people talked"
>
> Kevin Freiberg & Jackie Freiberg, *Nuts!*

Another example is Jungle Jim's, a store that has sales of nearly €100 million and a whole lot of laughs. The staff at Jungle Jim's describe working at the company in the simplest language: "We play work." Take a look at Junglejims.com and you will see how well they play business and have gone from a supermarket to a unique tourist attraction.

"Humour develops the habit of mind of seeing things
in different ways, of exploring possibilities."
Edward de Bono, *H+*

Humour is serious business and it starts with hiring the right people. When you use interactive advertising it becomes easier to spread your passion for the brand and then to hire from the base of fans you've created. Microsoft has always been a profitable company, but the fact is they've fallen far short of what they might have accomplished with a higher "cool factor" or an open source culture that allows customers to truly participate.

But it's not just about being ONE with one's customers, it's about a relationship where you share the benefits (better products, etc.) and share a common consciousness (yes, you read that right.) Hold on, are you ready for this? People share a collective consciousness – *a collectiveness* (Cardeña, 2008). I first ran into the term when I interviewed a number of professors of psychology. It means that sort of hard to define thing where you are about to call someone when that person calls you. What is often called corporate culture or the working environment of a company is nothing more than a sort of collective consciousness or collectiveness, something worth thinking about the next time you decide to update your corporate DNA.

Step up to the plate

The concepts behind the advertising game are changing; it's time to develop new ideas and concepts. Madison Avenue still controls a lot of communication money, but to take control of the changes that are taking place, they need to step up to the plate and hit the ball out of the park.

It's not about losing control, it's about incorporating
the force that consumer power offers.

Most big corporations don't understand that business cannot survive without evolving. Professor in innovation, Alf Rehn, interviewed pirates who copied other companies' products. One of their biggest complaints was that original brands where too slow to innovate(!) forcing them to start their own R&D and innovation departments. He also pointed out that as a fan of Apple, he had observed that less than three months before the iPhone was released he found pirate copies in China, copies that were actually better than the original (Rehn, 2008).

A while ago, a friend and I ended up dancing all night. At this disco the DJ put all the records along the wall next to the dance floor letting people dancing choose the songs. A good DJ is like good management, it keeps people on the dance floor. Why not put the records of your "business solution" on a wall so people will dance to your business? Today, DJs are fully portable with a portable music player, the new Pacemaker. They build a social platform at Pacemaker.net that actually creates a market they can sell their product to; they can "mix" social values with music.

Intel and Dell are two corporations that learned how to listen the hard way. In the beginning of the consumer revolution, they held on to an antiquated reality – they lost millions not listening to their customers. Today, they are more ONE with consumer power. They offer money to consumers to come up with specific ideas and build online platforms to interact with consumers "on the dance floor". They now understand that talent and passion are connected. As a result, they have started to build places to attract talent. Intel is humble enough to understand that their 90,000 employees worldwide are nothing compared to billions of talented geeks online around the world. This is why they have gone "geek hunting" - to find a new Google before anybody else.

> *"In an effort to stay on top of the latest software trends and cool new start-ups, Intel on Monday made public a Digg-like voting site called CoolSW, for "cool software." The site will tap the geek public for the most promising new software companies worldwide…"*
> Wired.com, 2007

If you not are listening to the market, you are simply losing market shares. On a transparent market, fans can easily start their own businesses that offer what super brands can't as I pointed out in my earlier book, *ONE*.

I recently met Patrik Almö, the CEO of Parts of Sweden, a company started by IKEA fans who wanted to take the IKEA concept a step further. The company offers add-on products and options that IKEA just didn't think of and it's turned out to be a winning idea. Small companies such as these can be more flexible and can offer low-volume solutions. They often have a more informal attitude, as you can see below:

> *"When you feel like you need a little inspiration or just want to "pimp up" your old IKEA furniture, pay us a visit."*
>
> Partsofsweden.se

Patrik points out that the worst thing that can happen is for IKEA to go out of business. IKEA on the other hand is thrilled – you can't buy Parts of Sweden's products unless you buy IKEA's first.

There are other IKEA "hang arounds" such as Bemz.com, which makes alternative sofa coverings for IKEA sofas. While they run the risk of being copied by IKEA themselves, they also provide a complement that both broadens and strengthens the IKEA brand.

How do you think a super-brand should deal with market share that they give away? I wrote in my first book *Detective Marketing* that 17% of IKEA's sales go to these hang-around companies, but today I'm convinced it's much more. How can other companies avoid a 40% "IKEA-effect"? Can they form partnerships with symbiotic companies? Could a computer game for IKEA Family members create e-brand loyalty? How about an online IKEA avatar for every IKEA fan where the distinction between the company and the avatar would gradually blur. IKEA could have real-life avatar meetings for their IKEA Family members or a Cosplay shopping party in their stores.

Doing business at the speed of tomorrow

News stories are often laid out around a clock to illustrate how they grow from a small lead to a big scoop. The *third party*, as media was often referred to in Ries's book, is today often called *old media* by the blog culture. The reason is that the digital world not only considers itself the newest, but also the fastest medium. The old media is often 48 hours behind what's happening on the world's blogs. And there are countless parallels to an old business and new business comparison. Seeing "today's window of opportunity" means at least being slightly ahead of one's time. People in extremely trend-sensitive industries such as fashion, develop an intuitive feel for what is contemporary:

> *"The present is just a confirmation that you've interpreted the past correctly."*
>
> Anders Arsenius, Fashion Expert

By the time a trend is big news, it's too late – you have to see it before your competitors. That's why I usually look at the market in different dimensions. Looking at the market in one dimension doesn't show what's before and after the present. I always look for patterns in the future by combining the history with the future; over the years I learn that reality is more 4-dimensional than one dimensional. Working in a 4-dimensional consumer relationship with the market creates an intuitive feeling for what is happening and what is going to happen. By combining this feeling with input from consumers you also have an opportunity to *create* what will be in demand tomorrow and adapt production systems accordingly. This can be compared to Barack Obama's successful political campaign. Barack Obama saw early on what people wanted and could therefore communicate to the roots what his coming grassroots wanted to hear and remember. Grassroots has no color. If you succeed with the roots in what you want to push forward, revolutionary changes can be implemented.

Östen Mäkitalo, the father of the mobile phone, told me all about his research from the 1970s (Mäkitalo, 2008). At the time, the Swedish telephone company told Östen that his research was a waste of time. After all, everyone already has a phone at home, what's the point? Today, there are some 4 billion mobile phones in the world, yet Östen makes it clear that his motto back then still applies today:

> *"It's easier to get forgiveness than to get permission."*
> Östen Mäkitalo, Professor, KTH

Apple showed us how slowly the mobile phone industry moves and how what passes for development is often just mutual copying. Östen is a humble man, but he would be the first to agree that visionaries often meet resistance for the simple reason that change costs money. (Of course, 4 billion mobile phones is also quite a bit of money…) Just think if there had been a way for Östen to bring consumers into the company where he was developing the mobile phone. He might have found support or at least inspiration from a few billion consumers.

When fans of the company are allowed in and take part in the story behind the product, it creates motivation within the company and word of mouth externally. This is a major reason why Apple now allows its customers to create programs for the iPhone.

The new trend is that trends are dead…

Today's trends are so fast and so specialized that the bigger players are going to find it harder to keep up and adjust their products accordingly (Arsenius, 2008). One solution is, of course, to stay ahead by living as ONE with the tribes that share a passion for your products. Today's consumer is often far ahead of, for example, software companies. By allowing more consumer input, these companies could save years of evolution and development. This is why open source solutions are leaving big companies such as Microsoft behind.

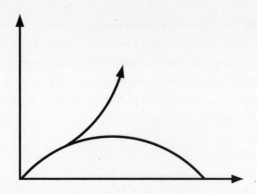

Östen Mäkitalo is currently a professor at KTH – Stockholm's Royal Institute of Technology. When I met him, he drew me a simple diagram of what happens when disruptive technology enters a market and product cycles are broken and replaced with something else. The demand for green products was strong long before anyone had heard of Al Gore. The same is true of all technical development. All the technology is readily available, but many companies are too "fat and complacent" about their market share to consider using it. It is often people at bit to one side of the status quo, such as Steven Jobs, who come up with an iPhone.

One technology that's right around the corner is Radio Frequency Identification (RFID), a microchip that is already being used on millions of pets, cars and the odd person or two. The military is already using it for personnel, while nightclubs in Spain and The Netherlands are using it for membership cards. The question is who will be the first to use it for marketing purposes? When will Tesco supply its VIP customers with these microchips?

Being able to promote consumption in 4 dimensions, opens a host of disruptive opportunities that can be taken advantage of long before competitors wake up to what is happening. By the time the market catches up, you've already moved on to something else. By developing this thinking along with the customer you create genuine credibility which in turn creates credibility for the brand (Arsenius 2008).

Many claim that man has come a long way. But often I ask myself the question: if the inventor of the wheel were to wake up from dead, what would he think of our progress? My guess is that he or she would not be especially impressed with that fact that, after countless thousands of years, our big accomplishment is that we can now choose what sort of rims we would like on our wheels.

From anti-advertising to the rise of advertising with consumer power

Once advertising addressed the masses; now, the masses are the individual. To reach a mass audience, you must now reach a critical mass of individuals with the message in order to spread it further. Every move on the market has to move you forward.

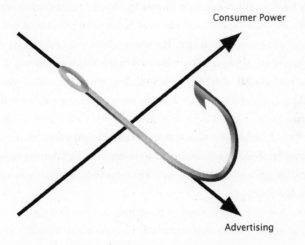

Consumer Power

Advertising

Now that the winds of change are blowing at their strongest, the advertising industry has a golden opportunity to reverse the general aversion to advertising, but only if they do it together with consumers, by hooking it to the enormous power of the consumer-power.

It's about taking the opera out of advertising

I have to admit, I have never been a big opera fan, something that changed when I got to know a number of opera singers. When the mobile phone salesman Paul Potts walked on stage on *Britain's Got Talent*, no one was expecting him (or anyone else) to sing opera on this talent show. The jury was stunned, the audience cheered and cried as this natural talent captivated the world. Opera has moved far from the life of the ordinary man who has difficulty seeing himself in the operas he sees. Then, when Paul Potts came on stage and held up the mirror, everyone could see themselves in this ordinary man. The general public experienced opera in a whole new way (I had the same experience when my opera friend created Mirror neuron.) Within a few days, the video clip from Paul Pott's world premiere was shown 28 million times on YouTube. The CD he released after winning the contest sold over 1 million copies in the first two months. Today, he is touring the world selling records, T-shirts and, of course, ring tones.

He has fans all over the world and his own site, Paulpottsuk.com, yet he has managed to stay true to the roots from his humble beginnings.

Interactive advertising can offer the business world the same sort of talent pool as programs such as American Idol. The business world is full of Paul Potts – natural talents without formal education. Advertising can attract fans, talents, products and innovation to the core of the brand.

Updating the conventional approach

Al and Laura Ries's book refers to a four-step process: Development, Research, Advertising and Branding - DRAB. This is how most business has worked for ages.

> *"Most products and services are marketed following a four-step strategy: **1.** The company develops a new product or service. **2.** The company researches the new product or service to make sure it offers consumers a significant benefit. **3.** The company hires an advertising agency to launch the new product or service with a "big bang" advertising campaign. **4.** Over time, the advertising builds the new product or service into a powerful brand."*
>
> Ries, 2002

They pointed out that the week link is number 3 – the advertising that, at the time, was too weak to find a place in the consumer's heart and mind. Their solution was to let PR build up awareness. Today's products and services deliver very low consumer satisfaction; most brands survive only because of a lack of competition. The whole four-step model shows that we need to re-think what advertising is and how we should work to be a part of business. In a time when the consumer is king, companies cannot rely on historical models that deliver mediocre results.

My short version of doing business with advertising

1. Do not produce a product or service in-house exclusively; bring the advertising agency in early. **2.** Be a detective on your market and become ONE with your customers – develop what consumers really want. **3.** Let the advertising agency launch the new product or service to smaller target groups to build and spread the buzz on the Internet. Let this stage be interactive to improve and adapt your product and service. Google.com introduced Gmail by letting friends introduce it to their friends (building a fan-tribe). **4.** Let the "big bang" advertising campaign go with full force only when it's relevant for both media and consumers. In this way, the brand building will grow like grassroots from seeds that consumers themselves have planted. It's more about building the brand from the inside out instead of with traditional mass communication from the start.

Advertising means business, if it is a part of the big picture...

Corporate management often has an education that is 20 years past its best-before date, while consumers base their consumption on what is happening today and tomorrow. The gap between decision making and the reality upon which the decisions are made must be bridged. In an age where the word interactive means NOW, advertising can easily be made interactive in a way that increases sales, as long as there is leadership and an organization that can deal with life in an age of two-way communication. It is only when there is real communication with the market that top management can be assured of getting the right information upon which to base sound decisions. I call this "real-time business". This is often not the case today, when many in management are relying on old statistics about what the market wanted yesterday, instead of finding out the market wants tomorrow. How exciting is the 100th iPod/iPhone copy to hit the market?

Poorly performing "top management" needs
interactive advertising to cure the fear that rules
in today's business world.

Today's big companies are often run by underachievers with spotty or out-of-date information. What's more, these organizations are often run on fear instead of innovation and vision. Management desperately needs to get in touch with reality.

If advertising can become more interactive, it will generate so much strategic information and send consumers on a tribal mission to change this gap (...and who can stop a mission?) Advertising must do more than just sell the brand and its products, it must help the tribe grow and become its ally rather than its enemy.

To put it in management-speak — advertising can be a tool
for minimizing risk and moving companies forward.

A two-way conversation is the best way to increase control while giving consumers credit as being more than just a collection of open wallets. One thing that needs to change, for example, is a typical homepage. Sites without interactivity are just a display window, while sites that involve the visitor are a door that invites him or her to come in. Nor have TV commercials developed significantly; the customer often has trouble seeing himself or herself in the picture. Who hands out business cards without a name and contact details? Yet this is exactly what today's commercials do. Commercials have become the world's most expensive business cards.

> *"TV interrupts two-way communication;*
> *the Internet is part of the communication."*
> Jeffrey Cole, Director,
> Center for the Digital Future

It is in this dialogue that company values can be developed into competitive advantages together with customers. If a carmaker introduces a car that is extremely simple and is developed with feedback from consumers, a natural buzz will be created and customers will bond with the car. It will be the car they'll buy with their hearts; after all, they're the ones who built it. The relationship grows from the process of participation and a tribe grows around that participation. When the car is finally manufactured, it is "based on a true consumer story". The advertising agency will then have the honour of delivering the new brand to the world, not with advertising in the traditional sense, but rather as a popular movement.

> *"80% is a good product, the remaining 20% is marketing.*
> *However, without a good product, marketing is useless."*
> Patrik Riese, Marketing Director, GM Nordic

Successful brands as Lexus, Singapore Airlines and eBay deliver customer satisfaction. With interactive advertising, brands can develop what they deliver to become today's superb brands. Unfortunately, most brands don't deliver what they promise.

Consumer power helps advertising function like swim fins by giving the message an extra push, but only if the message is built on what inspires and involves the consumer on his own terms. Once money was the only thing consumers were good for; now involvement can be worth even more in the long run.

Making sense in a world of tribes

Do you remember the names of your classmates in school? You probably do. These people were the most important people in your life for a long time, but why? You were a tribe. A tribe is one of man's best survival mechanisms by offering a rich gene pool. Some tribes can number a handful and others can be in the thousands – a far cry from your old classroom. A number of people on Facebook have passed the 5,000 friend limit while on MySpace some have over 70,000. When I first contacted the artist and blogger Tila Nguyen for an interview, she had about 30,000 friends online. I wrote about her in my book *ONE*, that she could combine her blogging with TV reporting at CNN. Today, she is very active on TV, although the channel is MTV – she is probably far too racy for CNN. On MySpace.com she now has 3 million friends.

"Human beings can't help it: we need to belong."
Seth Godin, *Tribes: We Need You to Lead Us*

Social networking media is growing exponentially around the world, even if not everyone knows everyone else by name. What is striking is that geographical distance is of secondary importance, especially for purely digital tribes. Why else would 20 million teenage girls meet and buy clothes for their digital cut-out dolls on Stardoll.com? According to the company's president, you will only understand if you're a teenage girl. What is fascinating is that the people on the site pay real money to dress up in a digital reality. Mattias Miksche, Stardoll CEO, tells how he once surveyed members with the question, "Which is worth more: clothes or digital clothes?" All too often the answer was that they didn't understand the question. Was there really a difference between the two? Mattias explained that for these girls, it is just as important to be as well dressed on the Web as it is in school. Maybe it is only the teenage girls who understand the truth: digital reality is for real.

With unique visitors in the tens of millions every month and sales figures higher than any department store, Stardoll.com is a reality that other companies might want to take a closer look at.

Just as you bond with classmates to form a tribe, so you bond with a brand, if there is an infrastructure for it.

All the superficial features turn us into pieces of a puzzle that
fit together and protect us from the outside world. There are
countless other "classrooms" in the digital social world.

Emphasizing external features (look at my hat in the photo) tends to
strengthen the feeling of unity in the tribe. When we mirror each other,
we want to get to know each other. Conversely, when outward appear-
ance is different it keeps others outside the tribe. My hat in the picture
could just as easily have been replaced with tattoos, motorcycles, games,
hairdos, clothes, music, blogs or other digital meeting places.

The need to find something different to identify as a tribe is also
present in the product itself. One reason that Saab fans like the car is that it
is different, an underdog with differences that reinforce its identity (Riese,
2008.) Uniqueness is also a success factor for customized Scion cars. At
Scion.com, a tribe of consumers is growing around building unique cars
together with a large group of subcontractors.

Getting today's brands to live in tribes requires an entirely different
approach. Instead of aiming directly for the wallet, brands must be part
of these kinds of tribes and let the tribes themselves shape the products as
symbols for their tribes and the tribes of others. This gives the products
a real function that moves boundaries for what consumers buy. Adidas is

trying with its Originals. If they succeed with their tribes, they will live on, even on the used market. On the other hand, if the commitment is only skin-deep and credibility is lacking, they may be in trouble.

For many brands, it's a matter of survival. The "shop till you drop" mentality just doesn't work in a time of melting icebergs and socially aware consumption. The purpose of a brand is changing from traditionally shopping to a feeling of belonging and other more human values. The customer will soon use his involvement with the brand as a form of payment as in the case of Adidas, where being part of the design process can be seen as a form of payment.

> *"More and more marketing money will move to digital media. It is there that you can interact and build a relationship with the consumer."*
>
> Patrik Riese, Marketing Director, GM Nordic

Tribes are not rational, but are often built on certain rational rules. One rule is being special. When a tribe becomes too big, new subcultures/ tribes will appear. This is especially striking in Japan where there is a tendency to find something unique and build a group identity around it. For example, believe it or not, there is a group whose passion is measuring the length of train platforms (Blom, 2008).

The point is that people inside the tribe understand the rules, but not those outside. A tribe is like having your own language and is as much about keeping others out as it is about communicating within the tribe. People have a deep need to organize themselves into scalable groups. Commercially, this means making yourself more relevant as an individual member of a group. This is why MySpace is opening offices all over the world: to be relevant linguistically, culturally and, above all, locally. Local content and authenticity means local advertising revenues.

Good, bad or indifferent, tribes are a way of creating levels of society. India has its caste system, the urban landscape has its dress codes, even Harley-Davidson has its code of authenticity. Those who ride their bikes without suspension are true Harley riders and lead the way while others have to pay for the bad boy image by buying Harley-Davidson accessories. This not only brings income to the brand, but also builds up the different levels of fans. Man has always built up hierarchies in this manner. (Of course, people can go too far, but then again, there are a lot of long train platforms to measure.)

When I interviewed MySpace's very charming Nordic Marketing Director, Jonas Nyvang, I was probably a little less charming (Sorry...) Jonas explained that there were then over 250 million members of which 11 million were musical bands. In 2008, the company had expected sales of $800 million. I questioned his figures; surely he must have missed an extra zero or two. After all, with membership close to the entire population of the US, surely the sales must be ten times higher. What I meant by my smart-aleck question was that with so many customers, his company had an enormous untapped potential in selling real goods and services instead of just advertising.

This is exactly the direction advertising is heading, especially when companies have the vision to see just a little further. Just think if MySpace could sell musical instruments to the 11 million bands that are present on their site? Or start a new record company based on a talent show model? As the interview got back on track, Jonas pointed out that MySpace will become more personal in the future making its way onto mobile phones (even though the Internet will always be the main focus). The site will also include other sites and integrate life with their site, that is, increase the opportunity for their tribe to live with their services.

Advertising as a no-brainer

The fact is that our brain has a fairly simple function – it keeps us alive. For this reason, positive messages are relatively unimportant – happy messages in advertising tend to be ignored as unimportant. On the other hand, there are not many brands that wish to be associated with survival of the fittest or dog-eat-dog. The brain makes things we already know automatic. We listen to music we "learned" when we were young. Even though different generations have different tastes, learning new music requires "unnecessary" energy when there is already so much old music stored away. The easiest way to bypass this filter is to create a new offer based on what you already like. Products such as the iPod didn't invent portable music, but simply a new approach to something people already liked. My personal opinion is that the reason both children and adults take in *stories* so easily is because of the way our brain organizes and stores information. A major part of this mechanism is word of mouth, a great way of organizing information in our surroundings, creating values and exchanging experiences for the survival of the tribe.

A no-brainer means having an offer so good that the customer doesn't even have to think. Our brains do not want to think if they don't have to; the brain already uses 20% of the body's energy as it is and instinctively does not want to waste energy learning anything new (Ingvar, 2008). So when people say that a certain advertising campaign is brain dead, it means that it is, in fact, succeeding. Or at least was, until consumers started getting smarter.

Brain research is very complex and is best left to the experts, which is why I chose to interview them and others who are trying to figure out how we work. An argument for positive advertising is that our brains have mirror neurons that cause us to smile when we are talking to someone who is smiling at us – a way of saying that we agree on something.

How is it, then, that we can judge a person based on first impressions, often accurately. In the stone age, the ability to make quick judgements was a key to survival, something that is still true. In my book *ONE*, I pointed out how brands should act as mirrors that allow customers (and employees) to see themselves. Companies are often afraid that consumers will become involved with the company and then turn against it if they disagree with some policy or if they feel that the company is not making proper use of their ideas. The real issue however, is keeping the dialogue constructive. The company can say no as long as it can explain why.

When I once sent a suggestion to YouTube, I didn't even receive a reply. In fact, a quick look at the site and I realized they had done the exact opposite of what I had suggested. Not much of a mirror for me as a consumer, yet they are so superior to other brands that I can forgive them as long as they're the best at what they do. That is, of course, only until someone else enters the scene with better service and feedback. Everything is a matter of competition.

Here's something to think about. The reason that so many films are shot in New York and Paris and not in Rapid Falls, is that most people can picture themselves in New York or Paris, but not in Rapid Falls. The first time I visited New York and Paris I already had a strong emotional relationship to these cities (Rapid Falls is probably a very nice place, but for the moment it will have to wait…). Brain research in mirror neurons indicate this is what forms the basis for man's emotional intelligence (Bauer, 2007) and is consequently very important in charging brands with emotional content.

> *"If everything were 100% rational, no one would*
> *ever buy a Ferrari."*
>
> Patrik Riese, Marketing Director, GM Nordic

Luxury brands provide a mirror for us to see ourselves as we would like others to see us. When our values change, so does the mirror. Driving a Hummer has gone from luxury to seeing people flipping the finger in the one's rear-view mirror. In our days of global warming, there is a growing dislike of cars such as a Hummer. There is even a site, Fuh2.com, with a collection of pictures and videos of customers making obscene gestures to express their feeling on the subject, complete with posters and clothing. Brand-wise, not keeping up with the times can be fatal.

As I mentioned earlier, the mirror neuron is important for the learning process and our ability to make sense of the world – we do what we see. I think that the mirror neuron is why we tend to be drawn to people who are similar to us – minority groups, motorcycle gangs, fan clubs and the like. We form tribes to survive and pass our genes on. Advertisers need to understand Homo sapiens' survival strategy to be relevant in a world of chaos.

Read the sentence below while frowning: *Pain is real; happiness is not!*

Now try reading it with a smile. *Smile and the whole world smiles with you* is true even for brands. Certain brands such as McDonald's and Shell can invest millions in corporate social responsibility (CSR) yet people will still tend to say their names with a frown. These sorts of companies have no chance of getting a smile if they don't actually change their corporate DNA from the inside. Now, try saying the brand you work with/for as you look at yourself in the mirror. What do you see? Are you sending double signals? The point is basic: if your customers can't see themselves in your brand mirror they will never be positive towards your company. This is why so many companies are standing still.

There are many tricks of the trade for making brands more whole, but in the end, it is the consumer who decides what he sees in your brand.

If advertising is to be a part of people's lives, it must add value.
People need an escalator to save them energy in life's long climb.
What do you have to offer them?

"Culture stones" that last

Back in the days of colonial India, English and Indian culture could not have been more different. The English came to have an enormous influence; they even got the Indians to play cricket! Today, Indians claim that the English part of their culture is disappearing more and more and Indian culture is taking over again. Yet, England will always be part of India as you can see in the Gateway of India in Mumbai. There will always be certain cornerstones; I call them "culture stones."

The Gateway of India is a beautiful culture stone that functions
as advertising in the context of its time and purpose.

Modern cricket has gone from a sport to a religion in India; it has become a far stronger part of Indian culture than of English culture. Differences in cultures can be strong as stones when they become rituals and manifestos of a new culture.

The same is true for corporate cultures in fusions. When Air France and KLM merge, or DHL and Dutch Post, there remain certain culture stones that will last forever.

What are the culture stones for your company? And can you share them with consumers? How can consumer values and relationships be culture stones? What is the most different combination of corporate cultures you can think of? Cricket is ONE with India – what else could be ONE over time in a corporate fusion?

Making sense of the world is what justifies the place of advertising in people's lives. One way to be accepted is to protect the culture stones that the brand wishes to be associated with. In 2007, I was in Prague, one of the world's most beautiful cities, but also one that needs considerable renovation. In the heart of the city, Škoda is being true to its local roots by renovating a well-known statue. Their advertising on the fence around the project is translucent allowing people to see the status of the work. "The revenue from this advertising is funding the renovation of this statue." For me, this makes perfect sense and seems like a natural evolution for advertising: to be part of something, to make a difference. Unlike sponsoring activities that have nothing to do with the brand, Škoda in this case is building a genuine brand. Škoda is building its brand into the culture stone of its birthplace.

How IKEA can survive the "Kamprad defect"

The "Kamprad effect", named after the founder and owner of IKEA, is the ability to create a culture where passion and genuine commitment is the motivation for building the company. This is certainly the case at IKEA and a number of other very successful companies. We have asked a number of IKEA executives what will happen when Ingvar Kamprad dies Everyone is a bit shocked at the question and we're a bit shocked by the shock. Ingvar was born in 1926 and, like the furniture he sells, has a limited lifespan. Five million people a year visit his 231 stores in 24 countries. Kamprad's life's work is impressive and should go on. But there is a risk that the Kamprad effect will become the Kamprad defect as the corporate culture he has built by force of will and personality can change.

Without Kamprad as chief and storyteller, the tribe's sense of purpose may disappear. With its 118,000 tribe members IKEA (IKEA.com) will be hard to manage without a strong internal culture. The effect may mean higher wages, more expensive shipping and lower sales at best. The worst-case scenario is that Kamprad is replaced by an MBA type intent on making the corporate culture as rectangular as the boxes it sells. IKEA stores are partially culture stones, but they could be even more unique. *How do you make the IKEA culture more concrete, more likely to be around in 100 years? What should an IKEA store look like?*

Building houses as advertising monuments

The iPod has become one of the major icons of our times; Apple has stretched the limits of how far a brand can go in shaping a culture. But why stop there? Why not build an iPad – an iPod house in Dubai?

Or why not build a tyre-shaped house? Another great idea for Dubai. The idea started at lunch with the designer Joachim Nordwall. We started napkin scribbling and by the end of the lunch, he was well on his way to producing some impressive 3D colour sketches.

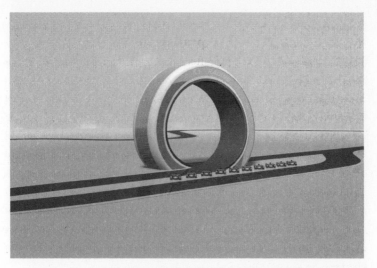

Joachim Nordwall, Jnrdwall.com is a talented and open-minded designer. After our lunch, he developed our concept into this 3D rendering. See more illustrations in colour at the author's site DetectiveMarketing.com.

The question is: who builds the building and who gets to drive through it first? By way of comparison: what is the Eiffel Tower worth for Paris – 25% of its recognition value? No one can put a value on those buildings that are forever competitive advantages for cities and regions. Although driving through the tyre building can be a virtual experience for everyone on, for example in Second Life, the real building could be headquarters for Goodyear, Michelin, Firestone, Pirelli, Toyo Tires, Dunlop, Yokohama or Hankook. There are so many brands to choose from, but only one can be the first – who will it be? It will be a screeching tyre start for whatever brand it is.

How can these kind of buildings become tribal homes?

Or why not build a house shaped like a refrigerator where the entire front of the building swings opens. Sponsor? Whirlpool. A building that moves once a day would be news around the world and a tourist attraction like the bells of Prague. Or maybe you could give everyone who buys a refrigerator a code to control the opening of the building? Of course it's absurd, but it's already practically a reality; there are already a number of buildings that are just one solid brand from top to bottom.

When companies buy the right to name a building after their brand x, it's called "naming". Naming involves a certain element of risk, however, when you use places that consumers already have a relationship with. Sometimes it's better to think twice before buying places as famous as Madison Square Garden in New York and renaming them just because you have the money to do it. For fans who have been going to these tribe monuments for generations it will generate mixed feelings (most brand managers don't want to have meetings with hooligans). But if it's done with a new building it can be seen as corporate social responsibility, a good way to tap into the local community.

> *"When these state-of-the-art stadiums and arenas are built,*
> *fans of all ages will spend decades cheering on their teams*
> *in a venue named after a (presumably) financially-robust*
> *corporate brand."*
>
> Brandchannel.com, 2002

It is also important to see the naming project over a long time period, at least 10 years. "Enron Field" doesn't sounds like a good idea today, for a stadium once called "Astros Field". Or, take the latest case "Minute Maid Park". Where Coca-Cola paid more than $100 million for the naming rights to the stadium for 28 years. Paying that kind of money and then getting a nickname like "The Juice Box" is not fun, but it's the fans who own the right to create nicknames.

> *Why stop there? Why not build a whole town that*
> *can become the best corporate social responsibility*
> *case in the world?*

Procter & Gamble City might have been an idea; Enron Town, probably not. The key is to find something to which you can apply the formula *Unique, Authentic Town × Brand*. A real Nike Town might be a good idea if it were based on putting back the socially constructive values that are all too often missing in sports today. After Beijing 2008, most sporting goods brands need to find a branding Dalai Lama who can put harmony back into the torch that burned a number of sports brands into political ashes.

I have a dream of building a town where everything is free, based not on charity, but on recycling... of people.

Let me explain. The town would start by taking people who are a bit down on their luck, perhaps out of a job and give them free lodging in the new town's centre. The town would be built on the same physical principle as medieval castles – based on rings. The first ring would, as I mentioned, contain people who need help, while the second ring would be full of those that can help them – doctors, psychologists, social workers, teachers. The third ring would be a mixture of socio-economic groups that could provide a stable, supportive environment that would increase the number of "inner-city" dwellers who would reinvent themselves and their lives and rejoin the world that they had at one time left, both emotionally and economically. The outer ring would be "professional celebrities" who would act as spokespersons for the city brand. The result would be thousands of new productive citizens, contributing energy to society rather than draining it; a brand that is promoted and a positive brand/company culture.

And there are endless variations. How about Nike Town, where everything is free and the pay-off is both social responsibility and a talent pool for future athletes.

The Walt Disney Company has built its dream town Celebration in Florida. It was a good thought, but the town is increasingly becoming known as "Weird Town" for its exaggerated tendency to quiet down all of life's more negative aspects – no one is allowed to die in a Disney branded experience.

Disney might well learn from France how death can be made a major selling point. There is a town in France where it is actually against the law to die. A smart mayor passed the law to put political pressure on the county authorities when the town ran out of graveyard space. The law activated not only the right politicians, but also the town's inhabitants who have taken the law to heart as a new lease on life.

The "fake factor" in facts

In Ries's book, advertising is referred to as art work while artists who work in advertising call it prostitution. The naked thought is that prostitution is about faking for money. Today, consumers are paying attention and money for what's real.

In real life when large agencies enter the viral market with fake amateur videos with million dollar budgets. Companies such as Brandfame offer product placement in amateur videos seen on YouTube. Companies such as Wal-Mart are paying bloggers to fake it. The results are fairly predictable: anti-fan sites and hate-websites such as Mitsubishisucks.com. In the case of Wal-Mart, there is even a full-length movie dedicated to an anti-Wal-Mart movement (Walmartmovie.com).

"People are the message when their intent is authentic."
Ben McConnell & Jackie Huba, *Citizen Marketers*

Easy to fake if the emperor is a nudist

Today's emperors walk around naked because they don't know better. They live in a reality where everyone is naked – most brands today are practically nudists. There is so much fake reality passed off as facts and research. This is the reality that forms the basis for the emperor's decisions. These companies proceed to build walls around their comfortable little reality. There are plenty of filters to keep out spam, but there are no filters for dissatisfied customers. When I tried to email the first chapter of my book *ONE*, I got the following response: "Mail Marshal (an automated content monitoring gateway) has stopped the following e-mail for the following reason: it believes it may contain unacceptable language, or inappropriate material."

The intended recipient of the mail also got a message that my mail could not be business-related because it contained the word "hate." For me it sounds like a joke: "Hey, how can we stop all dissatisfied customers who hate our brand x? I know, let's put up a mail filter and lock them out of our lives!"

> *All too many companies are using mail filters*
> *as a form of Valium.*

It is not the software that is the problem, it's the genius who formulated the rules for keeping dissatisfied customers from disturbing the company. But reality bites back hard. For the advertising industry, a business filter between consumers and companies can mean that market-critical information is lost. Is it any wonder that so much advertising is based on a false reality.

In movies we've all seen the line, "based on a true story." When will the same be true for other products? One way to turn products into true stories is to work closely with extreme consumers. In Stockholm, there is a man named Georg Carlsson, who has eaten lunch at the same restaurant nearly every day at the same restaurant for over 70 years. That's over 20,000 lunches. The value of George's lunches today is more than a million dollars. Just imagine going into a restaurant and saying: "I'd like to buy a million dollars worth of lunches." This week I talked with a gentlemen who has been drinking the same coffee brand for 60 years. Extreme consumers stay loyal even after death! Soccer fans of Hamburg SV are immortal and will be fans from their graves!

> *"Fans of the German soccer club Hamburg now have the chance for the ultimate resting place – their own cemetery and a grave covered with the original grass from the team's playing field."*
>
> International Herald Tribune

And, as for myself, I'm the third generation in my family to be a customer at the public pool I go to. I can't stop thinking of other extreme consumers and what they have been consuming over the years. What's your story? Have you heard about a loyal customer that is *extreme* in some way?

Extreme consumers are a great resource. They can give both management and ad agencies a feel for what is real and what isn't. Extreme consumers are a fantastic starting point for building a true story from the bottom up.

What's extreme today, maybe be average tomorrow. Not so long ago, one of the first cars made for female car buyers was marketed, the Dodge La Femme (1955-1956). Back then, it was considered extreme to build a car for female consumers, but today it's considered extreme *not* to think about women in marketing decisions. (Johnson, 2004).

Stealing cars with advertising

Modern technology has made cars too hard to steal without the owner. Car theft has centered around finding ways of stealing keys or getting the owner to get out while the car is running. But how do you best do this? Valet parking? When I was in the Middle East at the end of 2008, I heard about a simple, but innovative approach. This is how it works: when you back out of a parking space you see that someone has put advertising on your back window that is blocking your view. Naturally, you open the door and get out to remove it. At that exact moment the car thief jumps in and drives away.

But what if this was an advertising stunt for auto insurance or a new car? And what if the entire stunt were smartly planned with the husband, wife or family such as in the MTV show Punk'd hosted by Ashton Kutcher. The ethics are questionable, but the approach is definitely in line with today's advertising opportunities. (And lawyers will love it.)

Connect for real

A lot of critics say that advertising is prostitution. Well, let's say that you buy the services of a real prostitute and you guarantee that this prostitute will feel real pleasure. Don't you think that you would get a motivated hooker for a much better price? The same thing applies to advertising – everyone needs to get something from the transaction.

The time is over when advertising can fake brands into becoming real. Today's advertising has to build much more credibility right from the start. Even in the film *Crazy People,* the premise is that honesty really is the basis of success.

The VW Beetle was introduced as an ugly car, but a good one. The car was so different in and of itself that the advertising didn't have to do the entire job by itself. This is exactly how today's products and advertising should work together: the product/service should be part of the message. Consumers now have more freedom to say no to advertising. Yet, *No advertising* stickers on people's doors don't mean *no new products*. What they are saying is: "Add something to my life or stay out of it!" If advertising is to be a part of people's lives, it needs to make sense and add some sort of value.

> *For commercials that don't make sense: add explanatory subtitles or give the money to charity.*

In a media landscape where the most intellectual show on TV is *The Simpsons*, it shouldn't be hard to produce smart and interesting commercials (…but sadly Homer does not work at an ad agency). In other words, the entertainment level in today's television is generally so low that the entertainment potential of the TV commercial is wide open. Instead of saying, "Quick, grab your remote! You're about to see the same thing again and again!" commercial breaks could be more like little films where different brands work together as in real life. Many experts predict that TV programs are going to become more niche-oriented in the future and that the borders between advertising and entertainment will blur even more. Like mirrors, they will mirror the tribe's confirmation.

> *"Consumers are increasingly turning away from*
> *mass communication messages."*
>> Håkan Gustafsson, CEO, Carat Nordic

Instead of advertising going to Hollywood for "product placement", they should take over the entertainment business. Start by hiring Homer, Marge and the rest of the team behind the success of *The Simpsons*.

> *Forget television as we know it!*

Consumers now consume media on the move. The line between the picture and being *in* the picture is going to disappear. Passively watching television is boring for the up-and-coming interactive generation. The retail outlet is going to become the TV commercial "live".

Up until recently, the consumers have had a simple choice when it comes to advertising: you can run but you can't hide from it. Today, the shoe is on the other foot: advertising can run, but consumers *can* hide. That's why advertisers often hide the fact that it's advertising to avoid having to play that game that costs so much money. A transparent market offers neither the time nor the place to hide.

> *If you whisper, they will hear you better.*

Most companies only listen to consumers when they are in trouble, even though most of them don't even know when they are in trouble, or at least don't care. That's why companies can keep selling cars that are in fact nothing more than a refined Model T. Now is the time for consumers to take control of this evolution. The open source system is good, but it is not aggressive enough; we need "consumer SWAT teams" to open boardroom doors.

> The original SWAT: Special Weapons Assault Team.
> The consumer SWAT: Special Whispers Assault Team.

I don't mean that the change should be a violent one; the description is simply a way to add some real emotion to the bottom line. A brand is useless without consumers to take it to heart. So if you want a car that is more than a newly painted Model T and products and services that aren't straight out of a history book, you have to form your own positive consumer SWAT. Who will be the first to put up consumerswat.com to show how much whispers and word-of-mouth can accomplish?

> Be a part of the picture or don't bother.

Advertising is worth zero if it isn't part of management and business goals

Advertising will succeed when it lends colour to the client's bigger picture of how business should be carried out. If the advertising business is just about being creative for your colleagues, rather than building clients' bottom lines, it will disappear from the big picture altogether. The next step in advertising's evolution is to grow the industry into a sort of business media. This will make it easier for top management to understand how to buy it and grow with it. In other words, this book should inspire you to:

> Move business forward and drag top management
> along with you!

There is a risk of advertising becoming pure entertainment with no brand value. The Internet is a monster hungry for content and advertising can supply this content. This is great in the short term as advertising quickly goes viral and is spread to a large audience virtually for free. In the long term, the brand must be given its own content that makes it unique and customers must be given a chance to add their own dimension through interactivity.

> *"I tell all my friends to decrease their media budget and*
> *start working harder on the attractiveness of their offer."*
> Magnus Wistam, CEO, Grey Stockholm

Ideas and solutions:
Pampers sponsor sex?

A small town in Norway called Bamble is doing something concrete to solve an all-too-common problem.

> *"How much are you willing to pay for a few nights*
> *alone with the wife/husband for wild sex? Many*
> *countries and cities feel that their birth-rates aren't*
> *high enough and are taking drastic action to encourage*
> *families to have more children."*
> Adventuredad.com

It's a big problem for companies as well. Do you think Pampers could sponsor a payment for parents to make more babies and more consumers for Pampers? I have talked to a number of politicians about this problem, but most are too embarrassed to address it seriously. I did manage to slip in a recommendation that they could at least play more Barry White on the local radio (his magic voice has inspired the creation of more kids than most small towns have residents).

If you want to play piano, you have to listen to the music.

We can all dig up billions of dollars in the "brand graveyard". Even in marketing, death is life: interactive advertising can give birth to new brands. It's all part of evolution for brands to die and give birth to new baby brands. No brand lives forever, not even me. Genetics teaches us that this random change and mix of "genes" is good for long-term survival and development (Ridley, 1994).

There was a lot of mixing in 70s disco culture (and a lot of baby brands where born). Brands today live and die more globally than ever based on their genuineness or lack of it. In nature, the organisms that live on are those that reproduce. The same goes for products, brands and even MySpace. Companies don't want players that play for themselves; they want ad agencies that play for the team. That's why I think more clients are going to demand that the ad agency live closer to the brand. If these agencies get a percentage of the brand they will want to see more than awards on the bottom line. Some will say that ad agencies should not own brands they work with, but ownership makes them a sort of in-house agency that both knows more and cares more about the brand.

> *The reason so many brands die is that they try*
> *to compensate a bad offer with good marketing.*

In today's transparent market, faking doesn't work, even if you have the budget to buy all the media in the world. The reason is that the truth can spread for free on the Internet. For me, building brands means letting consumers be a part of the brand and filling the gap between what the brand offers and what they want. This is the key to an authentic brand.

> *"The body is merely an evolutionary vehicle for the gene"*
> *(Ridley, 1994). The same goes for brands; they are merely*
> *vehicles for their genes (offer, product, values, image, etc).*

Beyond Web 3.0

Traditional the Internet, with its screen and keyboard, is old news and an old user experience. Entire regions go online without computers – it's all about mobile phones. This changes everything from a business point of view and opens up new opportunities for advertising to become a direct part of the actual consumption. Today's advertising budgets are quite small compared with the total amounts spent on consumption in general. The retail and packaging sectors don't have the ad industry's visibility and flashy awards ceremonies, but they produce much more in revenues.

There are enormous amounts of innovation and creativity in all areas that lead directly to high sales figures. For example, the Smurfit Kappa Group is a cardboard manufacturing company that has sales of over €7 billion, results that speak for themselves. In time, the boxes themselves will actually talk to us as well – they have already more or less perfected a paper material that will store sound! A musician I know who has been having trouble getting his music heard listened to my advice that he should set his sights on becoming the first singing cardboard box. It now looks like he has succeeded in getting his voice "on paper" and the next time you open a magazine you may very well hear Anthony Mills voice.

These sorts of technological changes mean that the advertising industry must enter new areas such as R&D to give them more channels and better communication potential from the very beginning for packaging, paper and other products. As for mobile technology, these sorts of solutions make it easy to track the result of advertising and make it viable for communicators and ad agencies to work on some sort of commission basis.

By broadening your picture of what advertising is, advertising budgets will increase. In the digital universe, half the advertising is never wasted.

From Google Earth to Google Global Travel

Google Earth is a great service for seeing the planet in 3D even if it is on a flat screen (If Columbus had had a flat screen, chances are he would have looked at the earth in the same way. He probably wouldn't have set out on that badly planned voyage that resulted in the discovery of the new world.) I think the ultimate step for Google Earth is to connect people, not by using Nokia phones, but by using technology to help people meet.

Maybe Google Globe Travel could use this interesting prototype made by Igor Polyakov, Creative Director, Hot snow. Let's make the world a bit rounder with a computer (their service included).

Google is ONE of the strongest brands in the world. If its search brand goes into the travel business they have to do more than find the relationship between A and B. They have to help me discover a whole new world.

Let's look at an idea for how this Google Global Travel could work. Last minute fares are as attractive as a game lottery with few winners. Bad storytelling means bad business for the travel business. Here is an idea for becoming ONE with the world and making the consumer a new Columbus. As children, we've all spun a globe around, closed our eyes and put our finger on a random place saying "There!" Why not offer this as a service? Spin the globe and travel to a new place every time; sometimes it would be close and familiar, other times far away and exotic.

Be a Columbus and see the world for 900 euros.

All trips would have a flat rate of around €900 (the difference in cost will in the long run benefit companies offering the services). It could also be done on the Internet. Every customer that buys a trip will be given a globe (very retro and full of potential finger trips…). This kind of "game-travelling" would build and feed the story and also make the world and the service more round and real.

Who would be the first to offer such a service? Would you try it? How would employees feel about working there? Today, the world is in many ways still mentally flat. How could this service make it rounder? Perhaps the name should be Google Columbus. How would this service build storytelling? Could you combine travel and charity?

"Be who you want on the Web pages you visit."
Niniane Wang, Engineering Manager,
Google.com

Soon it will be possible to shop while you are sleeping. Your personal avatar can shop in places such as Second Life. Shopping will then become 24/7 and global when connected to Google Earth and let you travel to new places on earth and in space. (Next, the avatar world and the real world will come together as ONE, increasing the potential of Google by a factor of 99%).

Soon will consumers be able to drive down to Google's very own town.

From the Wild West to Google Downtown

The Internet has been nothing but the Wild West from the very start. It has developed at the speed of light, but not as fast as it could have had there been better revenue strategies. Advertising revenues account for some 99% of Google's sales. Yet, most advertisers are still not spending big money online. With more money, the Internet will grow like never before. The highways on the Internet lack direction and billions of consumers just don't know where to drive.

Google Earth is the first step to Google Downtown.

The search market is big online, but not offline. With technological changes such as mobile phones and broadband, this will change. Sooner or later, every transaction goes offline and it is here that you will find the really big sales figures. Most of Google's sales are still generated by less than by 1% of the total potential market. The online market is a small market compared to the offline market where we shop, eat and enjoy "real life". When we are driving in our cars, we use road signs to find out where to go. That road sign could soon become a new communication medium that "talks" with your technology (car/GPS, mobile, computer etc). I call it "Google Downtown." Old road signs don't know who you are. The new ones powered by Google signs could give you more relevant information because you can tell them about yourself – where you live, where you are right now, where you shop. The motivation to give this information to Google is to give you added value in life in the way of free mobile phones, the Internet and any other communication you could want.

Headlines are revealing, for example, this one in The New York Times (Markoff, 2005): "Google Bids to Help San Francisco Go Wireless." I think it is amazing how Google is never complacent for a moment; they are constantly moving forward. Their goal is not history; it is the future. Google is now moving into becoming an Internet provider and is trying to provide free WiFi to everyone in San Francisco.

> *"Our calculations show that a city-wide WiFi service can be offered for free in a city like San Francisco with a breakeven in 4 years... The same solution would be possible for Europe with cities such as Paris and London."*
>
> Maria Hellström, Group Manager, Cap Gemini

There is no such thing as a free lunch, they say. When you give away free Internet and free mobile Internet, you are paying for your lunch by providing Google with information about yourself. Every step you take is a search for something. Combining online and offline living is a bit like showing advertisers tomorrow's page in your diary. There is and must be a discussion about privacy issues (Cnet.com, 2005). If Google can add value to consumers' lives, however, they *will* give away information. Other questions pop up: can a computer ever be personal? Are road signs personal? No! Yet, in a way, they are performing the same function as Google Downtown might in the future.

Can this new version of the Google road sign provide us with information without selling out our privacy? Yes, I think so. Hopefully these steps will take the Internet from the Wild West to an orderly Google Downtown.

Road signs are not like pop-up banners, they have a function. You turn in because the message is important to you – a town, a shopping centre, a store. These signs are not like annoying commercial breaks in the middle of a film. They are part of the consumer's daily life.

Of course, not all signs are that easily understood, just look at Signspotting.com. Good for a laugh, but not always wrong if seen in the proper context. The "real life ad" will soon become just as natural as the Coke radio commercial – it is the context that forms the basis for the ad in real life, not the other way.

Google credit card

A thought would be to combine "Google Downtown" with a Google credit card that could change both the online and offline world and make history. Conventional credit cards can't compete technologically with the Google solution. Today's credit cards are little more than a modern version of cash. Google credit card will make the purchase a part of your own Google Downtown... and your life. Purchases can be dealt with as road signs, nothing personal, yet they will add value to the consumer's life. Where you go, drive and shop says a lot about you and can add value to your life if the technology behind it can add time, value and new offers (all depending on the information you provide the system). Consumers must feel that they're getting out more than they put in the way of information. This can then be developed into a community version of Google Earth. For example, when you are travelling, you can get tips on things that you'll like in the town you happen to be in at the time. Your behaviour pattern doesn't change just because you happen to be in a different place. As a bonus you get to know the people with the same interests in other places.

In this offline/online world, advertising can be more relevant and repayment time can be measurable in minutes instead of years. This, of course, can mean big money for Google and not just the 1% of the wallet they are getting today.

PART THREE

The Evolution of Advertising

In 1968, when Andy Warhol created his classic "15 minutes of fame", neither he nor anyone else knew that he was talking about the entire human race. If the history of the world were 24 hours, man's existence would only take up 15 minutes. Of these 15 minutes, the existence of the commercial is a millisecond. Yet it can be this millisecond that is the key to our future on earth.

Travelling to different places such as Dubai, New York, Bombay, Singapore, Brussels, London, Paris and Prague on business is like travelling to different evolutionary "time steps" of advertising. In the early days of advertising evolution, the artist painted ads to make the product "arty". This framework around the commercial message was an early version of added value. Soon, clients began to understand that buying art wasn't feeding the bottom line and they started to demand results for their money. This started advertising off on a process that took it up the evolutionary ladder step by step. Marketing is becoming more and more global and with it comes a corresponding increase in advertising expertise. To get business to take big steps forward I will suggest some way to move it forward with tools, methods and concepts. The steps will focus on the product, top management, sales and consumers to move advertising forward. When books with titles such as *The Last Generation* (Pearce, 2006) become bestsellers, it's time to reconsider moving the human race into space.

> *"We can see from ice melting alone that our civilization is in trouble."*
>
> Lester R. Brown, *Plan B 3.0: Mobilizing to Save Civilization*

Mother Earth needs a plan B, C and D. B for billions and C for consumers and D for demand. The world is far from unsinkable and full of melting icebergs. This triggers our survival instinct; we seek alternatives to our present way of living, regardless of the label in it. It is a fact that for those who find solutions with price tags, it will be as profitable as selling life jackets on the Titanic.

On the Titanic, the 1st class passengers were the first to be taken to the lifeboats just as it is the richest who will move into space first to save themselves from future disasters. On a planet that some claim is doomed, the biggest news story of our day is taking place every day. Katrina and a number of tsunamis are reminders that things are not right with the earth. Our survival instinct is a very strong motivator and has created an enormous market for green products and, in the crassest terms, a world of opportunity for companies that take advantage of the disaster scenario. Seascrapers, housing in space – a range of living alternatives are in the planning stages for 20-25 years into the future. The question that I often ask myself is: why are all these solutions so far in the future? The answer is that these things are already here – for a price. The price is too high for many; the currency is open-mindedness. I love our planet, but hugging a tree as the oceans rise 10 meters seems a bit absurd.

When the earth is threatened man will not go under without a fight or at least a plan B, C and D. No one talks about it, but a flooded world will generate billions in new business opportunities. What's more, these opportunities are starting today. Visionaries such as Richard Branson have an enormous advantage. When people start moving into space, he will have an incredible head start as he is already pioneering space tourism. As brain researchers are quick to point out, it is easier to take in new thoughts when there is something similar already in your brain. That's why it's important to sell space one step at a time.

One of those steps could be Moon Wine. Grown in soil enriched with substances taken from the moon, Moon Wine might be a good way of getting some space into both your body and your mind. Another sales approach might be to offer a space city on earth where the housing you buy includes a 50 year option on a place to live in space that can be exercised by your grandchildren with cryogenic immersion included at no extra price. Maybe it should be called Virgin Space Town (I wonder who would be mayor...?)

We may be living in the 11th hour, but a lot of people
are going to make a profit in the 12th hour.

Are you ready to leave earth? Sir Richard Branson has been ready for a long time. A person not confined by conventional limits will not be confined by the earth's gravity when there's a great big universe to explore. He is the kind of person who thinks outside the box and has managed to make it pay. Virgin Galactic is a commercial space line planning to offer non-professional astronauts the opportunity to travel in space. And why not – mankind has dreamt of space travel from the beginning of its existence.

If you need launching sites, you will find them all over the world. Why now? There are a lot of Branson wannabes who have a lot of money and want to take a walk on wild side. If you're a billionaire and have countless sports cars and houses and have been everywhere and done everything, then you are probably looking for something new. What's more, being able to say at a party that for your vacation you are going into space is a status symbol that few can match.

In the 11th hour, the issue of the survival of the planet has been discussed by any number of experts. One quote that has always stayed with me is:

"The planet has all the time in the world, but we don't."
Chief Oren Lyons, *The 11th Hour*

Three scenarios with billions of dollars, consumers and huge survivor demand

Green products are in great demand. People on the whole, however, seem to be having a harder time feeling good about buying low energy light bulbs when it seems that it's too late to make any sort of difference. The demand for space-living offerings is enormous and is now starting to attract the capital and the market to take off for real. Noah's Ark is on its way out into space. The space industry, which has always planned 20-30 years ahead, is ready for any number of scenarios. Visionary companies should take note.

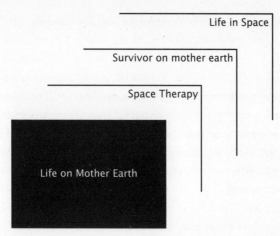

Man will look for new housing in space long before the earth becomes uninhabitable. Here the "out of the box" model (Rasulzada, 2007) has been transformed into an "away from Mother Earth into life in space." Forget all the super-brands on earth; space is open for new positioning in space.

1. **Space therapy**

   We need products that will mentally prepare us for the fact that our next move will not be cross-town but into space. (What moving company will you call?) This will influence fashions, transportation, furniture, food, development of new materials, etc.

2. **Survivor on Mother Earth**

   When the earth is flooded, there will no longer be enough land for the entire world population. We will need sea-based housing as an alternative to moving into space.

3. **Life in space**

   Living in space will be a fact in the near future. The level of uncertainty will make it as easy to sell this housing as selling lifeboat tickets on the Titanic. The first step is space tourism with Virgin Galactic as an example of a company with booked and paid tickets.

"If we want to continue beyond the next hundred years, our future is in space."

Stephen Hawking, Ted.com

By step two, many companies that have prepared for these changes will not only make out like bandits, they will also save lives. And when natural disasters arrive en masse, something only the military can deal with, they too will stand to make money as well. An army making money on not going to war will be a new concept. And suddenly the world will have truly green armies!

From positioning in the mind to positioning in space

I don't think it's possible to create a new super-brand such as Coke or Nike from scratch today on Mother Earth. It would simply cost too much money; there are too many other brands and too little shelf space. Space, however, is full of shelf space and has plenty of room for new brands. It's all about going from a position in the mind to claiming a place in space before it also gets too crowded and too expensive. Our minds are already halfway there – just look at the last 50 years of films – from Flash Gordon to Star Wars. We are ready for weightless shopping!

Moon Wine – a new brand, made on the moon

If you are going to start making a new wine today, you have to compete with half the world – from Italy to Chile, from Spain to South Africa. Finding something new to offer is difficult, especially as everyone already has a relationship with wine based on where it's produced. So what can we do?

Why not produce a wine from a place that all consumers are familiar with, yet one that doesn't have a culture and history that creates instant opinions. Add to that 12 hour a day worldwide visibility the moon.

moon wine

Have you ever thought of how the moon might taste? Maybe you should, but remember: don't drink and drive on earth!

I would call it Moon Wine and it would be the real thing! The wine would contain real ingredients from the moon and would be a sensation with wine critics all over the world. The first wine ever aged in space and old as the moon! For the media, it would be pure bottled BUZZ. Imagine, the first-ever space buzz – a brand that is reborn every night. Consumers will light up the moon with storytelling and buzz around the globe.

Look up. What opportunities do you see on the moon? How would you brand it, register it, trademark it? How is this product ONE with consumers and their surroundings? Is this the first product made on the moon? Will it make you feel like a UFO the day after?

What brands will be the first to capitalize on the space therapy on earth? How will this affect fashion, music, television, insurance policies...

The faster the ice caps melt, the faster the earth will be flooded.
Not a very positive thought, but also one full of opportunities. For example,
this cool Seascraper™ for an ocean-based bird house created by Cecilia Hertz
at Umbilical Design. The purpose is to show how we will live with
rising water levels in the not too distant future.

The first step out into space is for space designers to design housing here
on earth. I interviewed Cecilia Hertz, CEO of Umbilical Design, who
has actually designed spacecraft interiors for a number of NASA projects
around the world. I asked her about designing a space hotel on earth to
meet a future market – a hotel that featured weightlessness in elevators
and rooms, astronaut suits and the like. She lit up like a small planet and
answered, "Sure, it's feasible and it would be great fun as well. Not all
the technology is there yet, for example the weightlessness, but there are
a number of ways of creating a first-class virtual space experience."

Add to that a space shopping centre with the same sort of features as
the hotel. This mall would feature entertainment to build "space shopping buzz" coupled with guerrilla marketing on earth, such as hand held
shopping bags filled with helium to simulate weightlessness.

The next step would be to build an entire town, a "Virgin Space Town" where the mayor has to be Richard Branson.

As I mentioned earlier in the book, this could be a first step out into space – housing on earth with an option to move to space. With a little planning you could pay for your future in space today and I don't think there's any shortage of consumers who would pay generously for the thrill and cocktail party prestige that such a deal would offer. One way of making the offer more meaningful would be to offer a three-for-one package where you would pay for a space house on earth and get two more for free: one in space and the other in the free town I mentioned earlier – a house for someone who needs it.

Just think of having a house in space. You would be guaranteed to have a star or two right next door to light up your living room – both the galactic type and the Hollywood type. The real star is the deal.

In this new world, there will certainly be no shortage of entertainment and casinos, yet in space we might well see the hard currency of the earth in another light. We might suddenly realize that money has never been an especially good yardstick for measuring the value of things in life or an incentive for socially positive behaviour. The question is: how could we invent a new currency for the future based on values and involvement rather than gold? For me, the involvement and commitment of the customer is often worth much more than money. A thousand of the right sort of consumers can be worth their weight in gold, even in zero gravity.

Many people will be quick to point out that space is a far-off market both in time and in distance, but we are all already part of space. Often new opportunities are merely a question of acceptance. New opportunities are about having the mindset to tap a new potential.

And you don't have to go out into space to see new worlds of opportunity. For example, why not offer milk and Coca-Cola on tap in every apartment? This is what I suggested years ago in my first book *Detective Marketing*. Not too long after, Coca-Cola announced plans to begin distributing their beverage by pipeline. A notice in the *Sunday Times* article from March 18, 2001 read:

It may be just a pipe dream, but Douglas Daft, the chief executive of Coca-Cola, is planning to compete with water by channelling Coke through taps in customers' homes.

Interview by Rupert Steiner

There also seems to be a health trend that is pointing in the opposite direction: young people are turning away from soft drinks to healthier alternatives. Environmental consciousness is growing and people are reacting to the environmental impact of transporting bottled water when in many places, plain tap water is quite good. The Swedish gas manufacturing company AGA had this in mind as a new market and a way of getting closer to the needs of the consumer. The idea was to sell their CO_2 for carbonation straight out of the tap – home carbonation. The market potential is enormous.

In 2006, I was given the honour of lecturing to the AGA sales force about water carbonation right in your tap. Their ad agency Forsman & Bodenfors visualized it quite nicely.

Up until now, half of all advertising has been thrown away

The good thing about a boomerang is that you notice very quickly when it comes back. When I recently lectured for a taxi company I introduced the term "boomerang effect" – the idea that the customer should come back very quickly. If a customer takes a taxi from point A to point B he is creating an instant repeat sale in the form of a return trip from point B to point A. Naturally, any offer that helps create a boomerang effect can potentially double sales with results that are visible instantly. Is there a parallel in your industry? It might be a good idea to buy a boomerang and start practising. After a few throws you will soon see which money comes back and which doesn't. Almost all consumption can be compared to a taxi ride – it reveals what other needs the customer has.

The fact is that the second-hand trade such as eBay is the best thing that has happened to the retail business in a long time. eBay makes it easier for consumers to get rid of the things they no longer want and replace them with new products. This means that consumers are less afraid to buy the "wrong" technology. Today, it's easier to throw out old goods for the capital to buy new ones. This helps create a clear conscience for consumption which is great for modern consumers who, unlike their parents, do not want to keep the same furniture their entire lives. This consumer culture is a global phenomenon that is creating tribes linked together by consumption boomerangs.

> *"eBay.com is the world's largest business school for young people."*
>
> Magnus Kroon, Director of Business Development,
> Swedish Trade Federation

Consumption has many dimensions and eBay should easily be able to develop more boomerang effects and find both meaning and values in actively building the "business school" that their site offers. The way forward: recruiting (a monster of a market), relation-building and travel.

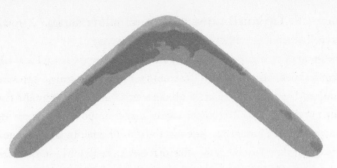

Up until now, half of all marketing has been wasted. But, as the old saying goes, you never know which half. With innovative advertising, marketing can become a boomerang with the potential of doubling the effect of the communication instead of throwing half away.

Returning to my taxi example, I find it incomprehensible that no one has seen the connection that people who take a taxi may need a car. Why not treat every ride as a test drive of a certain make of car?

One way of getting the most out of your boomerang is to throw it in new directions – for example, towards Bollywood.

> *"Moving is always a better alternative than standing still."*
> Pål Burman, CEO, Fairshopping.se

How to get 3.6 billion consumers to dance with your brand

For years, Hollywood was the place where the films of the world were made. Now there are a number of other arenas that are equally important. India's Bollywood is one of these arenas, one with an enormous audience. Brands such as Sony Ericsson have understood that Bollywood, which reaches half of the world's population, is an excellent platform for growing their brand. Yet, not many companies have understood the importance of adapting to such a strong culture instead of clinging to their own. If you know how to listen and learn, you can get 3.6 billion consumers to dance with your brand in a part of the world that's spinning and growing faster than Hollywood ever has.

On my first trip to India (it will certainly not be the last!), I told some people about a chain store in Sweden that sold only Indian products – Indiska Magasinet. Everyone looked puzzled and asked why. At first I didn't understand, it's easy not to see the forest for the trees. For me India was very exotic, but for the Indians it was just home. In fact, no one believed me when I said that the store actually existed until I showed them Indiska.com. Later, one cold January day back in Stockholm, I met the CEO of the company, Sofie Gunolf, who, surprisingly enough reacted much the same way. With 83 outlets in Sweden, it's easy to forget how exotic Indiska Magasinet really is. The phenomenon is not unusual. Many companies tend to tone down the originality of their corporate culture as they grow. It's only human nature after all – the human body is designed to save energy. If you draw a parallel between a body and a big corporation, you'll see that with age, walking is preferable to running. Although Sofie is far from old, she is the third generation to run this family-owned company. She told me about the company's beginnings in 1901, how exotic they were and how they grew to be the phenomenon they are today. The company now has plans to grow with new stories in locations where Indian is still considered exotic such as London, for example. And, more importantly – are you ready for this – they are about to establish themselves in India. As I am a big fan of Bollywood and the power of its films, I immediately saw how the company's authentic story as the perfect script: how the Viking fell in love with India, brought Indian goods home to Sweden to start a store and later returned riding an elephant dressed in the yellow and blue of the Swedish flag. Indiska Magasinet has brought India into Swedish homes for over a century with its clothing, furnishing, accessories and utilitarian spirit. Lately, they have expanded into Indian fashion.

I think it would be very interesting if they made modern jeans with Indian patterns or even down jackets. With their long, dark winters, Scandinavians need colour and spice more than the Indians themselves.

India has a middle class that's 300 million strong, all ready and willing to travel out in the world. Sweden is working hard to raise its visibility with this growing middle class in both India and China. Sweden is also putting a lot of energy into attracting more international film productions; earlier productions have been very effective in attracting tourists. A country and its tourists can be compared with a company and its customers – the key is creating a "ONE relationship".

Le Fuck Freud

In advertising, sex sells, yet no one has bothered to find out why. Not even Sigmund Freud, who established the extent of man's preoccupation with sex, but stopped short of its role in selling products. Sex is a simple, dependable Madison Avenue tool for reaching all social, national and political groups; it's primal communication with universal appeal. Modern researchers think about sex more in terms of survival, rather than as a superficial social phenomenon. This is not such a new thought, but revolutionary nonetheless.

Most big online brands are offline on what drives consumers to them.

Scientists will tell you that sex is meant to pass on and to strengthen our genetic material. Two people pool their genes for a new and hopefully stronger mix. For long-term survival, however, the gene pool must be bigger – at least the size of a tribe of 20 to 40 people. The tribe has become part of our most basic instincts – we even form tribes online, tribes that number in the millions. Tribe-building, something that sounds so ancient, is stronger and more important than ever. Unfortunately, the advertising industry has been slow to catch on, relying instead on copying and increasing media budgets. People dancing on the streets and in nightclubs often pop up six months later in advertising, often too late and after the trend has peaked or has ceased to be unique. The response from the ad industry has been to create lame viral marketing and copy other digital phenomena.

Advertising can't afford to imitate life, it has to be part of it.

The car industry has sold cars with bikini-clad women across the hoods for a long time, but they just don't sell as well as involving fans on their own terms. Today, it is all about supporting the genuine message that the fans offer the brand. GM, for example, supports Saab community events in Europe and the US that attract 20,000 to 30,000 fans. By supporting the experience and the sense of community, the relationship with the brand is strengthened. Saab contributes with Saab performance team exhibitions that are so extreme that fans are only too happy to film and post them on YouTube, reaching an audience in the millions. Saab has nothing to do with the film production; it wouldn't play as genuine in the digital world. The drivers of the cars are not professionals hired for the event; they are Saab's own engineers on their free time and passionate about the brand. In this way the external and internal brand have a chance to grow together into ONE. Saab simply supplies the tribe a forum; if that forum is good enough they can take care of the rest themselves. By getting close to fans and listening to their communities, brands have a chance to improve in weak areas before dissatisfaction sets in and negative rumours start circulating about the product (Riese, 2008). It's all about living in the present in a digital world.

> *"To create virtual products, you have to live*
> *in a virtual culture."*
>
> Peter Blom, Game Expert, Jadestone

Do you feel how the earth is swaying under your feet?

Try it. Stand still and you will feel the earth is swaying under your feet. The reason is that we are all on the same boat and the name of it is the Titanic. With all its melting icebergs, the world is no longer unsinkable. Often when I hold lectures and talk about "green money" I start with this example. When the Titanic started sinking, the people aboard had a "high level of awareness" that something was very, very wrong. We are starting to reach this level of awareness about the environment thanks to a number of wake-up calls such as Al Gore's film, *An Inconvenient Truth*. Our natural survival instinct gives us a great deal of awareness, very quickly.

The first brands that will go down are those that don't listen to the same warning signals as the consumer. So what should brand managers do? Start swimming? (Well, a bit of exercise is always a plus…) But there are a number of examples of how brands can tap into "green money" and float for a long time. (Good advice doesn't rock the boat by faking green at a time when the consumer's awareness is at an all-time high).

A new market economy is emerging as a by-product of over-consumption.

In a world of over-consumption, many people are looking for new values. The transparent digital world means that the advertising industry must rethink if they wish to be part of this new journey of discovery. When celebrities such as Britney Spears and Michael Jackson crash in spite of massive fame and fortune, it is a sign to their fans and others' fans that perhaps being happy has nothing to do with being rich and famous. This puts brands in a whole new perspective. When we are looking for meaning, we need brands that are part of our lives. Brands that live in the here and now create meaning in the midst of global warming. Many brands leave a bitter, artificial taste in your mouth – greenwash has always been hard to swallow. Instead of investing in becoming a part of the natural evolution of life on earth, they are more interested in a quick one-time sale, a one-night stand. Consumers can skip the first step in the consumption chain altogether when they see that it has a negative effect on our planet. After spending time asking IKEA personnel about a certain product, the modern customer can go home and order the same product on eBay. In other words, aware consumers pressure companies to make their corporate DNA a part of the earth's evolution.

Certain brands have a strong, natural connection between the sender and the receiver from the very beginning. American Apparel, for example, is an alternative to clothing made in the third world. All of its apparel is "Made in Downtown LA". By being part of a very local community, they hope to do more than just reach the grassroots; they also want the customer to see himself or herself in the mirror of their brand.

To act ethically when doing business, we need new business models. Here is a suggestion for a new type of consumer stairway, a four-dimensional perspective that acts as an antidote to counterbalance overconsumption. On the surface it may appear anti-commercial, but the truth is that customers just don't want brands that fail to offer meaning of some sort.

In the building where I live, I've seen a new phenomenon developing. Everyone puts things they no longer want in the hall. Everything is put in one place, so the anonymity of the owners is assured and everything is labelled "take me". The items can be everything from clothes, a sofa or an iPod to shoes, a table or 50 DVD's, all in good condition. It's generous and creates a neighbourly atmosphere, but why do people give away hundreds of euros of goods? It might be that people don't think it's worth the trouble selling these things on eBay or it could just be they are in a hurry to get back to consuming new things. Admittedly, our building's little custom can have some comic moments such as when you run into a neighbour wearing your clothes or when you're at a neighbour's and you're confused by the sudden change in furnishings. In the middle of a consumer desert, we've suddenly created an oasis of collectiveness. (In a tribe, we see ourselves in each other.) Charitable organizations could learn a thing or two from the above example – the relationship between giving, visibility and participation in the charitable act.

Trendy brands such as Diesel clothing, actually recommend that the customer combine their clothing with used clothing. Why? Because it helps their customers create an original look. It also raises a seldom asked question: why is there such an enormous difference between new and used clothes? After all, the car industry has succeeded in making it seem natural for the same car to belong to many owners in its lifespan. Why is it so difficult to create this mindset for other products?

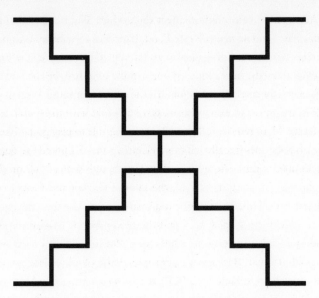

Towards the middle, the consumption becomes second-hand,
even though it remains the same brand. Most brands still only
work with visible communication, when it is the invisible
communication that has the greatest effect on the brand.

By letting the stairs have both a visible and an invisible dimension, you
get an overview of the entire consumption cycle. Many brands start with
trendy early adopters and end up in second-hand stores or on the homeless. By taking a more active part in the life cycle, for example, when a
shirt has changed owners for the third time, the brand can become a real
part of the tribe's existence. In the diagram above, there is no right or
wrong; it's open to interpretation. Trial and error is the most beautiful
thing in business.

    If you manufacture bicycles, go to Bikefurniture.com, a company that
makes cool furniture from old bikes that the customer sends in. So how
does this affect you as a bicycle maker? What is the big picture? By seeing
what is under the surface instead of just the tip of the traditional iceberg,
countless new opportunities present themselves.

All types of consumption affect each other. The music video game Guitar Hero and its sequel Rock Band, have had an enormous impact in raising interest in learning to play guitar. The electronic revolution that has decimated the music industry may, in the long run, be the best thing that's ever happened. Never before has the interest for music been so great; it is just the music industry's business models that have to be updated.

Guitar Hero removes all obstacles to being able to play guitar like Jimi Hendrix, but does it really sell more electric guitars? I posed the question to a number of music stores that sell quality brands such as Gibson (Karlsson, 2008). The answer was yes, the sales of Gibson and Fender copies have gone up. This, according to music store owners, is the first step. You buy a copy, learn to play a bit and then long for the original. Another dimension is that the original copies itself, but still makes a retro version of its old original. But perhaps most interesting of all is what is referred to as *signature label*, something I call *customization cloning*. These are copies of famous musicians' old guitars – exact copies complete with scratches, dents and cigarette burns. Everything on them is authentic – including dirt and finger prints from years of use. People happily pay €6,000 for a guitar from a well-known musician even though they can't play a note.

When these two trends meet, maybe one of the leading bands can introduce a real guitar with a Guitar Hero-like interface that lets you play for real.

I think there's a Guitar Hero for many other businesses, an unconventional product that can remove obstacles to the consumer using your product like a star. Getting close to the customer, in other words, makes it easier to differentiate products and sell them to those who are or want to be like the customer. For the guitar industry, this might mean that guitars could become like watches and glasses – you have several that you use as the mood strikes you. The closer you get to the consumer, the wider your offering will become.

Of course, the question remains: what can Fender and Gibson learn from 11 million bands on MySpace? Probably, that it is easier to sell to people who can't play but who want to, than to people who already can.

Pay-to-stay at Hilton prison?

It sounds like a joke, but it's not. I can imagine that going to jail is a terrifying experience, but it's also a commercial market. Prison business is big business in the US, with private entrepreneurs offering prison time as pay-to-stay. For as long there have been prisons, there has been an unofficial market for protection and luxury. The difference now is that the private sector is taking over. Will Hilton open prisons? Will you soon be able to check into a prison cell at a Hilton hotel? After all, Paris Hilton has already introduced the brand to prisons.

> *"Most people who have the resources, who are middle class,*
> *are so terrified of going to county jail that they would spend*
> *everything they have to guarantee that they're going to be*
> *in a safer environment."*
>
> Prisonlegalnews.org

With slogans such as "Bad things happen to good people," prisons are now selling their "extra services" upfront.

> *"For $82 a day – book a cell in a five-star jail."*
>
> Nytimes.com

This could all have been predicted when looking at the situation in 4D – commercial forces will always push to increase their sales. And, naturally there are the moral consequences. How will this affect the crime rate? Morality? Police work and its effect on the private security sector?

However, the 4D model is open to interpretation. Play with it - it is the most important piece of know-how, experience (or "anti-experience") you will get from this book – inspiration.

Buying new products today is as cheap or even cheaper than buying used. This means that charitable organizations have to rethink their approach. They can no longer simply collect things and sell them again, if consumers can easily buy new things at lower prices. Charity should therefore become a part of the business cycle. Many companies don't see themselves as charitable organizations, choosing instead to make altruism part of their corporate DNA. Yet, it is in the interests of most companies to acknowledge that over-consumption in the west can result in an anti-shopping backlash. In this sense, it is simply less expensive for them to be good than evil. An anti-shopping wave can hit the world economy hard and fast. We can see, simmering under the surface, a growing demand for consumption that makes a difference (or *non*-consumption that makes a difference.)

Production of new products takes time – a new car model takes 5 years, a new engine, 2. This means that when the time is ripe, it is hard for GM and other carmakers to produce environmentally-friendly cars that the market needs. If they had taken the time to analyze the changes on the used car market they would have seen what was coming years earlier. The consequences are that there is no shortage of SUV's gathering dust at dealers around the world. Before GM started to play catch-up with for example its SAAB Biofuel models, they had already lost years of sales. In a time when consumer behaviour is changing quickly, it is not only a matter of catching up; it is also about not giving away consumption to other buying behaviour such as alternative transportation. The auto industry has an ace in the hole – the powerful emotions that have been nurtured for an entire century, emotions that can still save it.

The music industry has been less fortunate. Their reluctance to embrace the digital age has meant that they have more or less lost an entire generation that barely knows how to buy music legally.

> *Being too far from changes in the market*
> *just costs too much…*

Many contemporary designers are using vintage clothes as a base for their designs while some large chains are starting to sell used clothes. Yet, the two are more or less the same phenomenon – the evolution of a brand. If a brand can survive through all the stages of a product's lifecycle, it will retain a presence where new trends are created. One way a brand can take advantage of this, for example, would be to sell a shirt with a three time buy-back guarantee. Let's say you buy the shirt for €70, the store buys it back for €25 in good condition if you buy a new shirt for at least €50. This means that the store makes €120 and can sell the used shirt again. This sort of system would build a strong sense of brand loyalty and community. If the guarantee includes giving the shirt to charity the third time it is sold, it would send out positive signals and help to counterbalance the over-consumption that plagues western society.

We return our bottles, why isn't there a refund on other products as well?

H&M designed by Al Gore

First, Hennes & Mauritz grew their brand with designers such as Lagerfeld and Viktor & Rolf and artists such as Madonna. I think the next one should be Al Gore. Working with world-class designers – he could help to make sustainable fashion and fashion sustainable, a sort of "We are the *design* world" that will also save it. The campaign would stretch all the way from the grassroots level to a global shop infrastructure with H&M – letting the consumer participate in a way he could never do while watching a movie. Naturally, a percentage of the proceeds would go to a green cause or causes, but money is only one of many dimensions that change the world. The suppliers of sustainable fashion and the trendy designers could take trips for a better mutual understanding about the total impact of their work, seeing how the clothes are produced and where the materials come from. In turn, H&M could use material from Al Gore's film in their advertising to send a message to the fashion industry: survival is not a trend!

Fashion is, for many people, a way of saying who you *are*. Buying Al Gore Fashion at H&M is a statement about what you *believe* and how you are changing the world for the better. But why stop there? With the right approach, this could easily become a movement. Every piece of clothing, for example, could include a password to use in Second Life. Or H&M and Al Gore could create a new version of Second Life called *Real Life* – your password would give you an avatar in this world as well. If H&M put an RFID chip in the garment, consumers could connect with their computers and become an avatar in "real life". As long as the consumer can control what the chip is doing, he won't think of it as a spy chip. For me, this is Web 4.0, where we connect the Internet with offline. Your personal avatar means that you are online wherever you are; you can be given a mission as in the game World of Warcraft. But this quest can also be offline, walking around town with your Al Gore designer clothes. It can be a mission from other avatars or a mission direct from Al Gore to save the world for real! In the control panel you can choose what happens when you walk into an H&M store. What kind of service would you like? Who would you like to talk with – Madonna, Al Gore or a "special avatar shop assistant"? Would you like to hold a lecture about sustainability in the store? Design a shop window or stand for a day as model in it? You might remind the store of your birthday or Earth Day.

So my question is: would you like to join me in a catwalk for fashion with H&M and Al Gore? This could be a big catwalk in the media or marathon catwalks that stretch from our cities to the environment we all want to save.

Transparent clothing by Google, Nudie and Al Gore

The IT industry is often more open to new ideas than the fashion industry. If H&M doesn't take my humble suggestion to go green, Al Gore could work with an IT company. Let's say that Google wants to communicate that they are delivering a transparent world. With the help of fashion designers, Al Gore could produce socially responsible, sustainable fashion. The clothes would be completely transparent as a personal statement about the naked truth. A "naked" Al Gore on the catwalk would generate global press coverage. The consumer could choose what level of nudity they prefer or the level of statement they would like to make. It would become a modern tribute to the modern tribe.

For the Swedish brand Nudie Jeans, transparent clothes would mean the "real nudie" deal. They have already shown their commitment to social responsibility with their organic denim; Al Gore could take their brand with him around the globe.

> "Nudie is the" naked truth about denim". Denim has the
> ability to age beautifully – formed by its user into a second
> skin, naked and personal."
>
> NudieJeans.com

The clothes would be a boon to global tattoo culture, creating a new public audience for their work even in winter in cold climates. Pickpocketing would rise, but Al is a smart man and I'm sure there's a way to minimize the problem. For the prudish, being naked might cause cultural clashes, but then again didn't we come into the world that way? Now, when nature needs to step back to survive, we can all become role models for saving the earth. Can you picture it? If not, look at the photographer Spencer Tunick's artful photos of naked crowds. (If you would like to sign up for his photos, just fill in your contact information and skin colour at spencertunick.com).

Everything is relative and so is the myth that advertising is stupid. I once held a lecture at a high school for gifted students that were not gifted with humility. They complained how stupid they found advertising and that they would never buy those "stupid brands" I had named. I stopped the lecture and walked around in the audience to have a good look at what they were wearing and guess what, I found lots of these "stupid brands". These were bright kids and they all laughed at my point, yet as gifted as they were, they still didn't understand that we are not a logical race. The point is that you don't really have to be especially smart to learn how to outsmart advertising. It's a skill to be learned like any other.

A skull brand named Cheap Monday

Back in 2000, two friends here in Sweden opened a second-hand store in Stockholm. They quickly built a thoroughly modern story with a skull logo that hit the market when consumers walked a sort of customer catwalk of real life with their unique look (The €40-50 price tag for their jeans is also great storytelling.)

Today, their consumer catwalk has taken Cheap Monday to 28 countries with over 1,000 stores in Europe, the US, Japan, Australia, Canada and the Middle East. Check out how modern sensibility meets common sense in a skull at Cheapmonday.com. I think the brand Cheap Monday should be Cheaper on Mondays so the brand can deliver a little more on its name promise. Regardless of what day it is, this is a brand that knows how to hang on to its first loyal customers.

"A brand that grows too quickly can risk losing its core of early adopters who consider the brand to be theirs."

Adam Friberg, Founder, Cheap Monday
(Willebrand, 2007)

In a lecture given by Cheap Monday's co-founder Adam Friberg, he explained how their business plan was visualized with dancing apes to the tune of €50 million in sales. Many people laughed at this joke, but not long afterwards, the company was bought by Hennes & Mauritz for €100 million. As Cheap Monday had moved in on both the cheap modern jeans segment and had taken over some prime retail locations, the buy-out was a smart move by Hennes & Mauritz. Smart, but not Cheap. They did miss one little detail – they should have bought them on a Monday. A little humour can be quite profitable.

A lack of humour, on the other hand, can be expensive for a brand as Apple learned when it lowered the price of its iPhone just after many early adopters had bought them at almost twice the price. The headlines hurt the brand, even with the company's attempts at reimbursement.

Jeans have always used sex-appeal as a selling point. Bongo Jeans, for example, has always used a certain star's tush as a symbol for the brand. Yet, there is still a certain amount of objectification involved.

As for girl power, the tickets to the Spice Girls' reunion concert in London sold out in 37 seconds. Over 1,000,000 fans bought tickets. Girl power is a force to be reckoned with.

When many people unite against a brand, a demand for an alternative is created. It is in many ways trendy to be against something, probably because it is a natural way of making a strong statement about who you are and what you believe in. Brands have become our way of talking with each other and we all want to say something and be someone.

Customization is an optimal version of differentiation for many brands. Here is an idea for Levi's Jeans. "Levis YOU" – new jeans bursting with *your* creativity. The jeans market continues to grow with ever more styles and colours. When I talk with salespersons in clothing stores, they say that the variety of jeans is directly related to consumer demand. Years ago, Levi's made jeans so popular that they even made the cover of a Bruce Springsteen album. But today the product is more 'undercover' than 'on the' cover. The number of jeans brands on the market is a challenge that great advertising cannot meet alone. Companies who produce jeans are faced with the challenge of making their jeans stick out. Here is ONE idea of how they can work with consumers.

Why not offer jeans consumers a sewing machine and some paint at retail outlets? Why haven't the producers of the sewing machines and textile paint colours tapped into the jeans trend? Consumers of today want to be individuals and not have the same jeans as everyone else. The market is wide open to colour and personalization. Levi's could tap into this individual trend by designing their ONE version of a sewing machine that doesn't look like it belonged to someone's grandmother. This new machine could not only sew, but also paint. It could be connected to the Levi's site and MTV for new patterns (you see a music video and it instantly produces the jeans in the video.)

When you upload your own jeans design to MTV, maybe the next time they show the same music video, Bono in U2 would be wearing them. This added-value would increase their bottom line and create a direct connection with consumers. It would make it easier to find talented new designers. To inspire new patterns, this new sewing machine could also be connected to maps at Google, so you can use your own street map as a jeans design (and find your way home late at night…). What map would you use on your jeans?

In Beverly Hills, there is a new store called Fashionology LA that understands that fashion is about personality and that brands should offer real individual value. That's why they let customers (mostly teens) make their own clothes and even design them. When their friends ask where they bought their clothes, they can answer that they designed them themselves at Fashionologyla.com. Great storytelling and a great way to tap into the 4 dimensional steps that build buzz. Letting consumers spread the word by being a part of the story is smart and fun in a time when YOU are the centre of the world. The next step could be to let the designers sell their creations and become a sub-brand to Fashionology LA.

> *I once saw a movie where the grim reaper asked a person*
> *if he was ready to face death. "Can it wait until after the*
> *next Super Bowl?" he asked.*

Advertising is as much a part of the Super Bowl as football. The commercials are often made just for the game or at least to be released in the context of the Super Bowl. We need more "Super Bowl time". Every commercial should be specially made to fit into the context of the show where it airs and become part of the "entertainment package."

Try saying to your clients or your agency that you're going to turn your next commercial into a Super Bowl moment. Unlikely, but it's worth a shot and at worst you may end up with better advertising. Every time people get together for something special, the advertising should be just as special and worth investing time and money in.

> *"Brands have to incorporate a brand platform that fully*
> *integrates the five senses."*
> Martin Lindstrom, *Brand Sense*

Product + body = impact and consumer involvement

In a time when the world is getting more global and confusing, the human body has become more universal. In a world with hundreds of languages there is only one human body. In these days of increased terrorism and the heightened security that comes with it, biometrics is a growing field. Biometrics is a technology that identifies people by their bodies – face recognition, fingerprints, DNA, hand geometry and iris recognition. ID documents can be faked, but biometrics can't. A number of commercial players are already using this technology, such as Disney World that is using it to match tickets with ticket users. A boon for security, but also for advertising. The body of the customer can interact with the brand, the advertising, the product or the service with more than just a tattoo. It is easier to create genuineness if the consumer feels the brand physically. Apple, a part of your body; Harley-Davidson, vibrates your body; IKEA, builds up your body. Now it's advertising's turn to understand these principles. Advertising can be a physical experience. From the skin-deep advertising of the past, advertising must take the next step to create involvement at the gut level.

Hire fat people in health food stores

When you want to lose weight, who do you trust: perfect genetically skinny people or healthy chubby people? I would trust those people who have managed to lose weight themselves. "I know what I am talking about" doesn't mean anything without a physical track record. It's like Japanese food – you're convinced it won't make you fat because Japanese people aren't fat. So why not apply the same principle in health food stores?

Let's say you hire 2,000 fat people (check the wording of your ad carefully with your lawyer…). Take photos of them together with consumers in your stores and some sort of time stamp to date it. Then put up these authentic photos in full size behind the counter personnel at the check-out. This way the customer will know that the person he or she is talking with knows what it means to lose weight. Some people may think this is a bit too much, but they haven't been fat. Drug addicts don't trust people who haven't been through the same thing as they have. That's why so many people working with rehabilitation have a substance abuse background. Common sense, right? So why should fat people trust skinny people?

If you're buying a book about losing weight, you'll probably have more faith in someone who is fat - Dr. Phil for example. The rest are too skinny to trust, unless they can prove they were once fat.

What is the advertising potential of a scale that not only tells you your weight but also senses when you are over your ideal weight and shows you the best products to lose it? You could even connect the scale to the Internet or give the scale away free as advertising for a company that has pledged to help the US population lose 2,000 tons of weight in a collective health program sponsored by insurance companies. A campaign like this could be worth its weight in gold or, even more valuable, worth its weight in word-of-mouth advertising!

Make the consumption the commercial

Life used to be so easy for the advertising industry. You made a TV commercial and everything was taken care of. Today, consumers are searching for their identity in a more fragmented time and are living in closed tribes. Advertising must learn to cope with this new fragmentation. It is less expensive to reach out to the world where the customer is right now. The moment that he is making a purchase offline or right after is the cheapest, most effective and least expected moment to make an impact. The bored consumer is the new nirvana. Dead time is golden time – on the plane or the bus. Just as the transaction is being made, that transaction can become a commercial for something else. Hilton could, for example, distribute blankets on airline flights with "I'd rather sleep at the Hilton!" The door to a baggage claim carrousel could be painted to look like the back of a Mini, a simple and elegant way of talking about baggage space in a small car (Viladevall, 2008).

For Starbucks, airplanes have also figured into their marketing as a way of following the customer out into the world. The company discovered that a flight is a good and unexpected place to get a good cup of coffee (Simmons, 2004). (I like to hold management lectures in the air, but that is a whole different story.) The main thing is the mental journey. I want every flight to take me beyond my destination, just as I hope this book takes you beyond yours.

We can expect to see much more advertising in the public space. By taking on more artistic qualities, advertising will be able to claim a larger palette. Creating credibility will motivate many brands to work more closely with artists in the same way as Absolut Vodka. I would call the mix "Artisation" or something similar (yes, I know, we really need a better name…). Some call it artvertising but artisation is for me when the advertising itself become the art.

Toys will be a part of kid's bodies in the future

It sounds like science fiction, but the toy industry is right now looking into how toys can be physically connected with kids. This means that kids don't need to use their hands or even their eyes to play with these toys of the future. But why? The answer is that children are more open to new things; they want to be more extreme than their parents were at their age. As toys are BIG money, toy companies have the resources for research. They know they need to fill the gap between "old traditional toys" and "computer games." Kids are the wildest and fastest target group on earth when it comes to BUZZ around a new product.

Evolution and revolution are connected.

Let's look at a futuristic idea for the introduction of new toys. Let's say a new Harry Potter film is about to be released. Five hundred kids in each of the world's 200 biggest cities are invited for the premiere. They all sit down together with reporters to share the experience with the rest of the world. When the children enter the cinema, they get a new toy that connects directly to their brains. When the movie starts, there is nothing on the cinema screen; everything is coming from the new toy machine directly into children's senses – a total illusion. Kids aren't watching Harry Potter, they are a part of the story and can choose to be Harry or anyone else in the story. If they would like to see the film as a game, they can choose their level of interaction with the movie.

Reliable unnamed sources tell me this kind of research is being done today. I won't go in to all the complicated ethical issues; it is a dangerous road, where fantasy and reality are easily blurred. But, at the same time, some evolution theories claim that Homo sapiens won't survive if we don't develop or at least cross-breed with computers (!)

Today's toys are "anti-creative".

When I was a kid, I didn't always have the toys I needed to play a certain game. I used chairs as cars and made do with whatever else I could find around the house. I believe this was a major factor in the development of my imagination and why today I work with workshops on helping CEOs "play" on new markets. When I was young I automatically thought "out of the box" because all too often a box was all you had. In contrast, when you go to a toy store today, you will find a lot of boxes locked into a "build this model only" concept, with a handbook completely free from any trace of imagination. The result is that we're creating a generation that is going to need a handbook for everything.

Today's hot products are tomorrow's museum exhibits.

If new toys hit the market with a built-in connection to kids' brains, tomorrow's workplace is going to be an interesting and creative business atmosphere. This technology would quickly make today's computers, mobile phones and other products museum exhibits. For most of us it would be the same situation as the grand old lady I was talking to on the train yesterday who told me: "I just couldn't believe that the television was real when I first heard of it. Real moving pictures at home!"

When will Harry Potter release this kind of "brain connected" movie? How will it affect computers and mobiles? Is this a marketer's dream, to build top-of-mind brands inside our heads? What do you think of the ethical issues of these toys of the future? What do you think of the lady on the train? What were your favourite toys? Did your toys help you think creatively? McDonald's distributes more toys than anyone on the earth – how can they better combine commercial needs with ethical issues?

iGore + Live Earth = Walk the talk to music

Nike + iPod are made for running, but why not make them walk the talk with music. Make them do more than just make music together at Live

Earth. Why not build a liveearthwalk.org where green fans can join together for a green walk to work – compare your steps with famous people such as Al Gore, Leonardo DiCaprio, Madonna and get green points that are connected to the sponsors of the Live Earth Walk. Great for the earth and great for your health.

The next step could be to develop a pair of shoes that double as metal detectors. Just think: every time you take a walk, you can discover treasures… or avoid environmentally unsafe areas.

Taken or single?

Many successful companies pop up as the answer to a simple question. One such simple question was: "If you wear a ring to proudly show that you're married, why isn't there a single ring?"

The answer became a successful international company – Singelringen, "the single ring". When you buy the distinctive turquoise ring they make you are not only buying jewellery but also admission to an international singles community. A great idea, although I think they could take the concept one step further by taking a cue from another Swedish innovation.

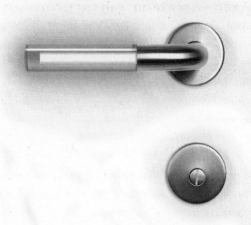

Designer Alexander Lervik created a handle for public toilets that shines red when occupied and green when free. If you can build a similar functionality into the single ring you could very easily change the status of your ring from *single* to *taken*. The ability to change the message on your ring would be great PR and create great word of mouth. For example, who will be first celebrity to change the colour of his or her ring live on The Oprah Winfrey Show? Or why not an entire TV show connected directly to the ring? Who is single and who is not - just think of the possibilities in trying to get people to change colours. Even weddings could be part of the fun - the ceremony would be very much coloured by the colour of the rings of the people attending the ceremony.

Make no mistake, singles are big business at every level. Singles are a very profitable target group for many companies – they spend more on housing, cars, etc. It's not by chance, then, that the grocery store chain ICA has opened a store for singles. ICA has over 5 million visitors a week, more than any nightclub anywhere in the world. Just think what a little toned down lighting on Friday night could do to let single rings glow single green or unavailable red somewhere between the vegetables and the coffee. Naturally, we could go digital and send out single-signals via Bluetooth or the Internet, a sort of virtual perfume.

Axbo – a wake-up call for technology

Axbo is an alarm clock that wakes you when your body is ready. It is connected to your body and has a unique function.

> *"With Axbo you can wake up in your optimal sleeping phase identified by a unique wake-up algorithm based on body movements."*
>
> Axbo.com

There are so many products coming out now that are connected to the consumer's body. An extension of the "Nike+iPod trend", these products are taking this thinking to the next level.

How can this be developed for cars, airplanes and apartments? When will someone offer the Axbo alarm clock for free if they can wake consumers with their sponsored brand?

PART FOUR

Filling the Gap between Advertising and PR

The missing testicle

In the old days, French aristocrats believed that by having their left testicle amputated, they would only give birth to sons (Ridley, 1994). The same thing is true for PR. By itself it will not produce what clients need. When the amputee aristocrats discovered the error of their ways, they probably killed the "cleaver consultant" that came up with the idea. It is not a good idea to amputate market PR; one should instead get it to work alongside with advertising. We need both; two genders are good not only for the survival of Homo sapiens but also for brands.

Good results are good motivation for change

Money rules the world, they say, in consultancy as in everything else. Many of the experts I have interviewed have pointed out that it is the client who drives change. If a client wants change, he'll get change. Clients are getting better at putting together their own dream team from different disciplines that are then given set goals. This allows everyone to focus on the business value that is creating profits for the client. The ideas become more important than the structure (Uggla, 2008). Regardless of the medium or area, the key is being both committed and relevant (Hoffstedt, 2008). Connect communications goals with business goals, let it have management-level priority. It is simply a matter of identifying the goals clearly and then opening the doors to give everyone a chance to affect the results.

> Point towards the results and the change will
> move in that direction.

Money won't change the world they say, but it sure makes it go round. And in the end it is consumers who provide business with its money. As long as you keep your eyes on the consumer, everything else will fall into place. Fans of a brand have the passion and time to inspire both marketing and innovation for any brand willing to listen. Marketing is at its best when it spreads to all departments of the company. Even if there is a marketing department, R&D and customer input are essential to the big picture of today and tomorrow. It is all about profit, yes, but profit is made of passion, the driving force of innovation. As dealt with in the milestone book, *Crossing the Chasm* (2002) by Geoffrey A. Moore, mixing disciplines pays off if they are connected to the tribes who want to be involved with the brand and spread the word. Mixing advertising with PR is a good way to start spreading that word.

No matter what labels you put on the different areas of a business, it is what the consumers do that matters. The buyer side of the transaction is always the key. What's more, you have to keep in mind that many things influence a brand, many of which you no longer have control of (Grahn Brikell, 2008).

> *"Our idea will be something we know nothing about today.*
> *That's why we must keep an open mind along the way."*
> Sorosh Tavakoli, CEO, VideoPlaza

Being open to change is a key to success. Openness to different disciplines, seeing history as an asset and the future as a challenge is what will steer clients in choosing their partners.

Changing structures are gradually filling the gap

At first, the media was overwhelmed by the speed and emotional intensity of community that 100 million bloggers had to offer. The result was a loss of advertising and consequently a drop in revenues for a number of players. But media is quick to catch on and has, just as I suggested in my first book, used new technologies to build an infrastructure between the sender and the receiver of the market communication. In my book, I wrote about how CNN could develop a mobile phone with Sony to enable people all around the world to become reporters. This is almost exactly what happened, only it was Nokia and the client was Sweden's largest daily newspaper, Dagens Nyheter. Yet there's still a long way to go in changing the paper's attitude towards the reader. The reader must be allowed to become more of a sender of a message, yet also remain the receiver, in order to create a community feeling where he can see his mirror image in his tribe. Here, there are already a number of tools such as Twingly.com, a site that connects news articles with blogs that write about those articles. This in turn increases advertising value and creates a win-win situation for both parties, increasing both readability and circulation. The same is true for online ads and films that can link on to the advertiser's site. It's a matter of involving the visitor and extending the experience to create a stronger relationship to the brand and sales. CNN has built references to YouTube and Facebook into their broadcasts and has even introduced their own social platform, iReport.com, where consumers are the reporters. Today's media success formula can and will change even the biggest player on the scene.

Google knows that the media buys search words linked to breaking news that will soon be in great demand. The reason is simple: they want to capitalize quickly on the increased traffic that these words will generate. For example, a news item about David Beckham can generate all manner of traffic for, say a ticket agent or a gossip magazine (Honkamaa, 2008). It all comes down to turning news into advertising – not exactly a new concept, but an increasingly important one, especially in a world where new generations are growing up with new media consumption patterns. Or, according to Jeffrey Cole, the director of the Centre for the Digital Future: "When a newspaper reader dies, there's no one born to replace him." In this time of change, advertising is taking on a new role.

In earlier US presidential elections, the less the media wrote about the various candidates, the more advertising was purchased (Ericson, 2008). This commercial rule of thumb changed in the latest election when Barack Obama's digital word-of-mouth approach won over some 2,000,000 people who joined his campaign. Regardless of whether you're talking about an election or a brand, the channels to communicate a message are today very fragmented and are no longer controlled by the few, but rather by the many. When the media landscape changes rapidly, both the consumer and the media consumer can move their consumption online, which then becomes a channel for the established media as well. News agencies in Norway, for example, have begun citing companies as informational sources. This often gets lost in the shuffle or removed when the information goes on to other media, even though many consumers would appreciate knowing where the facts originated. And there are other factors involved. In many countries, advertising is subject to advertising taxes while editorial content is free. What's more, many companies that are restricted from advertising a certain product in a certain way – for example that sugar is harmless – are free to sponsor "studies" that can later be released as "news".

Filling the gap with tools and models

Innovative thinking is the key to finding a wavelength to reach today's more segmented markets/tribes. Those who succeed in finding the right wavelength of advertising become more effective, only if the receiver of the message accepts it and sends it on.

As you begin your journey into the future, you have to nurture a sense of play and think "differently or die". Yet being unique as an end in itself is of little interest in business. The key is to be different in order to succeed.

> *"...being different for the sake of being different isn't enough. An identifiable target market must value the difference for it to be a candidate for your Core Message."*
> John Jantsch, *Duct Tape Marketing*

Persians invented chess to train their warriors to think strategically. Staying on the "advertising square C4" no longer creates enough bottom line business for clients. Today, advertisers need to develop ideas that move business forward by playing on the entire chessboard.

When I interviewed the chess master Roy, he won in less than 8 moves every time. I understood that he had a winning strategy...

When I played chess with Roy, he dominated our chess game by using the four squares in the middle of the board – they are the key to both defence and offence. Roy is unique. He has no ambition to be famous, only to win. For someone like me, his unique method of controlling the strategic squares is devastating.

In today's fast and changing communications landscape, it is essential to know which squares are the most strategic. A chessboard consists of 8×8 squares. 64 in total – a very complex situation with a lot to take into consideration (An interesting coincidence: Bobby Fischer, the American chess legend, died at 64.) Just as in Sam's chess strategy, advertising is all about dominating the 4 most strategic middle squares and influence how a business develops in the market. The 4 squares in business are retail, distribution, products/services and relationships. Once upon a time, big established players could afford to lose in the short term to come out victorious in the long term, but today the short term is often the same as the 8 moves it took Roy the chess master to finish me off.

We need more chess players

For companies such as Enron, WorldCom and Exxon, the problem is neither advertising nor PR, it is that they have a message that few find appealing. Genuineness and authenticity are seriously lacking. In normal companies, however, advertising and PR cover the entire chessboard, not just a couple of squares and add an entire new dimension to the company's business idea.

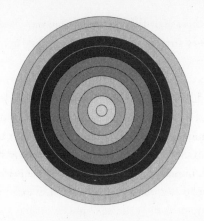

Authentic smaller companies find it easier to see the strategic chess squares. As they are closer to the customer, it is much easier for them to react to the needs of those customers and get "free market information". Closeness helps management become ONE with the market. For large companies, this means creating very local retail targets. The number of targets can be very high, yet the potential pay-off can be much higher. Not only does it give the company closeness to the market but it also creates meaning, pride and local identity for the company's employees. Both the sender and the receiver of the message see themselves in the mirror (Mirror neuron). This more personal relationship creates understanding for differences in local consumption, traditions and values. The money invested takes on a human face and is associated with specific products and services.

The shapelessness of the head office is replaced with many distinct smaller images from the local markets. Merely knowing a little more about what is happening on the street, where people live and work, what they think and what they want, is worth millions in involvement and enthusiasm. This is especially true of global companies who prosper when they can find the right balance of tapping into the local culture while maintaining their own unique identity. Combining the flexibility of the local company with the resources of an international one is a winning formula. It's all about knowing which chess squares are most important globally, nationally and around the corner.

Here are a few factors that determine how the
chess pieces should be moved…

Unique Selling Unique (USU)

In a time when customization is growing faster than ever, it's time to update the old model of Unique Selling Proposition (USP) to Unique Selling Unique (USU). When I Googled USU today I got no hits, so the time is right. In relationships, we search for the perfect match – two unique people who become a couple. USU is a more personal choice than a USP.

Consumers want to buy brands that are unique and make themselves unique. The Internet is full of companies providing uniqueness to consumers. A rapidly growing Swedish company, Shirtstore.se, sells uniqueness in the form of limited-run T-shirts – they guarantee that they will only make 50 of each T-shirt design. Can GM give you the same guarantee that you are unique? Yet there are many cases of big companies offering USU: Adidas, GM, Zildjian, Fender, etc. How USU is your brand? And how successful can it become with USU?

> *"In a marketplace of me-too offerings, people don't seek*
> *features and benefits so much as tribal identity."*
> Marty Neumeier, *Zag*

USU case: tribe drives eBay to success

In 2007, I met Tamara Gielen from eBay who was one of the speakers at an email marketing conference. One thing that was clear to me was that the sender/brand and the message must be the same or you will probably not connect with the receiver. eBay for me is more of a tribe than a traditional brand. Tamara pointed out that consumers who do business on an international level tend to be more loyal to the brand. I think this is because different local tribes that connect and help consumers see the bigger picture. One of my close friends has tribe friends in Norway, Japan and Great Britain because he sells spare parts for classic English cars (and earns more money on eBay than at his daytime job). For him, eBay is his connection to a tribe and in the long run I believe the tribe is more important than the spare parts he sells.

> *In today's digital world, no brand can exist without*
> *a solid base – a tribe of fans, a fanbase.*

Less is *amore*

A quick way of getting to the core of what customers value is to get to the core of what you are actually offering. The old saying "less is more" is even more powerful today. Mankind has some very complicated needs, the most important of which is to simplify life. We all have a need to build an aquarium in the middle of the sea. On the Discovery Channel, I recently saw that when we are in love, we tend to use less of the intellectual resources normally devoted to critical judgement. Not coincidentally, this suspension of judgement is a success factor for many of today's digital social networks. Creative types have long used "less is more" as a guideline to make their work more appealing and easier to take in. I call it "less is *amore*" – the love of USU is what consumers want today. The more you focus on the unique, the easier it is to love the object/brand. The more unique a brand becomes, the more "real" it must be. Closeness makes consumers more open to what a brand stands for. Passion makes us more open; advertising should spread this passion.

> *Many people build pools with a view over*
> *the ocean. This may be a visual expression*
> *of what makes communities so successful –*
> *you see the wildness of the ocean, but you*
> *can enjoy it from a small, warm, safe pool.*

From bonding to
"debriefing branding"

The world has become harder to understand after 9/11 and a little more frightening. The reaction is to build communities, tribes and aquariums with bulletproof glass. With the rise of religious fanaticism, there is a hunger for the more positive aspects of faith in a more humanistic and western package – spirituality without the danger. At one extreme there is the "Disneyfication" of religion. Books such as *A New Earth* by Eckhart Tolle and *Eat, Pray, Love* by Elizabeth Gilbert sell in the millions and get a big push by the world's best book salesperson, Oprah Winfrey. All this is a response to a strong need to understand the world in a time of perpetual bad news, climate change and terrorism. All this is central to branding as well. Most branding gurus preach bonding with your brand to get closer to your consumers. Blogs work in much the same way – they make people feel good when they share life. On TV police series, we often see officers debriefing to deal with all the traumatic things they see in their work.

> *Today, I got no hits on "debriefing branding",*
> *but 53,600,000 hits on "bad news" on Google.*
> *Here is a gap just waiting for a brand to fill it.*

With all the war and terrorism in the world, today's consumers, in a way, see more in a week than a policeman did in a month a decade ago. All this 24-hour a day global "bad news" is hard to handle.

Today's media mix the deadly serious with advertising, rendering much of the branding meaningless. To make things even more confusing, as I mentioned before, the survival mechanisms in the brain tend to give bad news higher priority. In a "bad news" environment, brands today are desperately trying to bond with consumers and it can often feel a bit plastic. The result is that many brands are creating their own media channels to get a better forum.

Wouldn't it be better to offer what I call "debriefing branding" – helping consumers deal with all the stress and negativity around them? To do this, brands need to be REAL, take part in the changes in the world and be ONE with the consumer's life. Brands should not be spiritual leaders, but should in some small way offer a bit of meaning.

It is important to connect the values of "debriefing branding" with social responsibility. This means not only offering a way of coping with the world, but also a way of taking responsibility.

> *What contemporary brands can you*
> *think of that already work with debriefing*
> *branding? How do you think debriefing*
> *branding can make consumers handle life*
> *better in a REAL way?*

Balance tool for evolutionary
steps forward

A good tip: learn to use a balance scale as a marketing tool to find the right balance or create an imbalance that will help your brand dance!

Situation   **Needs**

Start working on your balance today!

Our need of products and services are reflected by this situation, online as well as off-line. If advertising can find powerful statements, it can avoid the feeling of meaninglessness of a TV commercial in the middle of news about a natural disaster. Yet, many of these jarring contrasts can be used to the brand's advantage. It's all a question of balance. For example, when my bathroom scale climbs above 100 kilos, information about gyms, health and dieting suddenly seem more relevant and when it goes to over 150, I start to see medical services in a new light. Perhaps a not-so-low-calorie restaurant such as Pizza Hut should find a way to balance the advertising medium with the weight of the individual. Perhaps makers of bathroom scales could together get together with the advertising industry to find a way to synchronize body weight with relevant advertising messages. For example, perhaps iPod and Nike might be interested in getting the slightly overweight out onto the street equipped with their products. And what wouldn't Coca-Cola Zero pay to reach 30 million fat consumers?

Second Life is becoming "real-life advertising".

Going uphill, the more horsepower, the better; but going downhill, it's the brakes that are more interesting. If you're talking to motorists, talk to them about brakes on the way down. Conventional advertising can reach motorists, but not in direct relation to their current driving situation. Naturally, running ads with wheelchairs on accident-prone stretches of the autobahn gets motorists' attention, yet it is still primitive, often unappreciated and far from the potential of what *could* be done communicatively.

For example, imagine if a brand such as American Express gave away free GPS navigators to their VIP customers in exchange for receiving advertising about hotels, restaurant and anything else of interest when travelling – all with a common denominator: the establishments accept American Express. This would make it so much easier for Amex to sell its cards to merchants. The sales pitch: how would you like 20 million millionaires using GPS to lead them straight to your hotel/restaurant/store?

AdWords, by comparison, are less direct and immediate. You need to be at a computer and remember the horsepower you needed in that uphill stretch a while back. Just think if you could activate the advertising in the middle of the hill, exactly when you needed it? What wouldn't that mean for an advertiser? This could be done in the free Amex GPS in your car. A simple press of a button would let the driver make a purchase or get more information. Perhaps you could even buy horsepower online – as soon as the transaction is made your turbo is reprogrammed and the extra power goes straight to the wheels just as you need it.

Real life AdWords.

Google could easily connect AdWords with Google Earth to make the connection between offline and online by giving you the location of someone who can give you more horsepower when you get back to your computer. The potential revenues from blurring the boundaries between online and offline are enormous.

How much would you pay for an airbag,
4 seconds before a head-on collision?

You're driving 120 km/h and your GPS screen sends you an offer: in 20 seconds you may have a head-on collision. Would you like an airbag? The price goes up €100 every other second until the last few seconds when it's too late… A bit of science fiction, yes, but the principle remains the same: real life, real-time AdWords.

Face the facts to succeed

To succeed you must be able to deal with the relevant and elegant criticism in Ries' book. The areas that were pointed out as weak points for the advertising industry must be dealt with: art, creativity, awards and credibility. Even if the times have changed to the advantage of the advertising industry and the disadvantage of the PR industry; it's still time for a change.

Animals have more fun in real life.

At a social get-together I happened to meet Marianne Eriksson, the director of communications of WWF Sweden. I mentioned an idea from my first book: just think if WWF could get every company that used an animal in its brand to take responsibility for protecting that animal in the wild. Ferrari would take care of wild horses, Jaguar, the Jaguar and so on. Marianne loved the idea and then went silent. Suddenly she said, "A good thing that the panda bears decided to go with us!" We had a good laugh and talked about how the pandas had long discussed their preferences for brands. One of them was quite keen on Arthur Andersen, but that little bear disappeared without a trace along with the brand.

The discussion started me thinking: what happens to brands that use animals that are endangered or on their way to becoming extinct thanks to climate change? Soft drinks and Vicks Blue both use a polar bear as symbol, an animal that can very well disappear from the planet. The image of a polar bear swimming for miles between drifting icebergs before drowning is perhaps not the best sales argument for a happy soft drink and an "extra strong, extra fresh" throat lozenge. I made a note to call these two companies to ask them what they are doing to stop the global warming that is causing the polar cap to break apart, endangering the polar bears living there. Or will they just change to a more plentiful species? Or perhaps a species that we are doing more for? (And remember, the panda is taken.)

In the credits to many Hollywood films you can often read, "No animals were harmed in the production of this film." I think it would be just as appropriate to write, "All the animals used in this ad have been protected…" or "Ten per cent of all proceeds from this product will go to protecting animal x …"

There are no shortcuts to the animal kingdom.

All animals in advertising are a kind of shorthand, a mental shortcut. Big, wild, strong – these animals are symbols and much easier to tame than group management or your average CEO.

Don't fill the gap with fake

In my last book *ONE* I wrote: "The gap between consumers and corporations is as wide as the Grand Canyon, full of missed opportunities just waiting to be converted into big business."

This concept applies to 49% of Apple's current total sales. The missed opportunity in this case was a consumer with an idea for a little product that was not a computer: the iPod. It took endless knocking before anything happened, but eventually Apple gave in and that little product soon accounted for half of the company's sales. Today, Apple is more open and is gradually opening its door more to be *ONE* with its customers.

More corporations are beginning to understand the opportunities in the Grand Canyon gap and are following in the footsteps of eBay, YouTube and Google – companies that have created brands, not by remote control, but by inviting customers in.

Then there are companies that see this happening around them, yet still prefer to hire a consultant to help them fake it. As a consultant myself, I often get invited to meetings where the CEO says: "I read your *ONE* book about how to be ONE with consumers. Can you tell me how we can profile ourselves to be more in line with this consumer revolution thing?"

> *The fact is that "fake" is a billion dollar industry full of struggling dinosaur companies…*

Companies who try to fake it are hanging on to a fake reality that will ultimately pull them down. Big bucks can be blinding both in business and in ethics. Selling dangerous, harmful or useless products just to make money has long been a sound business idea. Historically, it has often been easier to make money not caring. In a transparent market, however, companies can go out of business very fast if they get caught in a lie.

Even worse, this gap only grows wider when management decisions are based on old reality. The Internet has changed the way we do business. Many CEOs now helplessly ask their kids what the Internet can do for their business. Success is all about filling the gap.

> *Instead of trying to manipulate reality by framing reality,*
> *it is better to deliver real consumer experience.*

PART FIVE

The Future Looks Good

Shark bites are good
motivation

Man's history is full of examples of moving faster than our competitors. The laws of nature allow a species only so much leeway to adapt before a new species takes over (Ridley, 1994). This applies to advertising as well. It is better to develop as a business partner with both companies and PR agencies to help them move faster and to remain competitive. Remember: we live in an age where consumer involvement is more important in the short term than the money they spend.

To summarize, here are a few examples
of how the market is changing

Al Gore's green seeds are sprouting. When a message is unique, it tends to grow by itself. At the end of March 2007, Al Gore lectured in Stockholm, Sweden, planting green seeds in the media. Soon after, I saw the grassroots growing all over. Parked cars in Stockholm got "green parking tickets" for having the wrong tires. Cars with summer tires got a message on the windshield saying: "Thank you for saving the environment by driving with summer tires!" A positive message that spread positive buzz – this person is making a difference and so can you! Cars with studded winter tires got a handmade painted green sun saying: "Did you know that your studded winter tires are bad for the environment? Please change your tires. Have a nice day!" None of the tickets were from any specific sender – grassroots don't need one.

Consumer generated advertising is built on trust.

This really happened the week that Al Gore was in Stockholm; people suddenly felt that they could make a difference. So if you have a bit of paper lying around, you can recycle it into a green message today.

Why Michael Moore movies work as advertising for change

When Michael Moore was on NBC's *The Tonight Show with Jay Leno* to promote his latest film "Sicko," it was not only extremely smart PR, it was also a long commercial for change. The same thing applies to any other celebrity with a public platform – they combine advertising (movie/books), PR (mass communication) and the Internet to interact with their audience to change the world. Moore recounted an incident about a family that had filmed their own hospital story on YouTube with a note that he was free to use this story in the next version of *Sicko*. The effects could be seen fast: in a week the insurance company called the family and reduced their bill from $66,000 to $500.

I don't think Michael Moore would agree with me that his movies are a sort of advertisement. Still, the way he takes a complicated reality and simplifies it into a powerful message that strikes hard and fast is very much like a commercial.

In a fake world, people are searching for something real

When consumers think that everything is fake, there is a built-up demand for something real. The Ultimate Fighting Championship (UFC), for example, was born out of this longing. The president of UFC is Dana White, who understands how to turn fighters into real people and real brands and how to turn violence into sport.

Conversely, figure skating took off when sport was turned into violence. When Tonya Harding became violent it was a big tragedy for many, but it also opened up the sport to a much bigger audience and interested big channels and big sponsors such as Toyota Prius (Milton, 1996). The martial arts don't need a Tonya Harding (even if she belongs in a cage), they already have Viasat and Eurosport broadcasting both UFC and K-1. In a world where everything feels fake, these fights feel 100% real. Mixed martial arts (MMA) is full contact in a cage and is the most extreme fighting sport on the market (legally). There are now slightly outrageous clothing brands such as Tapout and Affliction are making their way into mainstream retail outlets. At the same time, brands such as Adidas are also getting into the sport as a way of staying on top and moving forward. They are quickly moving into the fast growing, multimillion dollar market: fight clothing for mixed martial arts. Stars such as Georges St. Pierre and legendary Randy Couture are good role models and are sponsored by Affliction. When it comes to quality, these consumers are extreme! For brands such as Adidas, this is a learning market that can be what punk culture was for other brands – a launching pad to new billion dollar mainstream markets. Today, the sport attracts big brands such as Adidas, Harley-Davidson, Sony PlayStation and Bud light beer (with the slogan: *Plays hard, drinks easy*).

These fights are often attended by tens of thousands of sweaty fans and martial artists, an excellent target group for Tiger Balm. Pain and sports are a natural connection for "the scent of Tiger Balm" - word of mouth can be accomplished without words if the other senses are activated.

The "Tonya Harding success factor" is not something to emulate, it should however, inspire us to think creatively about what extreme changes can revitalize a brand.

> *What can your brand do to increase consumer involvement and create a ketchup effect for radical change?*

PART SIX

Postscripts

How advertising can become "man's best friend"

The dog is a wolf that has been bred to be man's best friend. Advertising that chases consumers as prey is nothing but a hungry wolf. Can advertising be bred into "man's best friend"? It all depends on needs and social relevance which in turn depend on the attitude of the advertiser. Relevant advertising is often surprisingly welcome and can enter the consumer's homes through its own little dog door, just below the "No advertising" sign, but only if companies realize that marketing is less about who is the alpha male than it is about creating something useful for everyone. Our society is developing into a society where shopping is suspect along with the advertising that drives it. Yet, nowadays, advertising plays a role even after the purchase, even after the product has been resold on eBay.

The boundary between customer and producer will gradually start to blur as consumers change their consumption patterns; for example, when they start to produce their own electricity from their own windmills. Advertising will become more of a social force if it succeeds in becoming a part of tribes emerging all over the world. As the products become more secondary, relationships will increase in importance. We can see this trend clearly today when companies add a social dimension to their brands: music stores become venues for local bands, Barns & Noble cafés are becoming social showcases, etc. Soon, most brands will have their own versions of YouTube, MySpace and Facebook, all tuned to the right frequency of advertising for products, services and for being part of that particular tribe. Building tribes means having free media channels to reach consumers directly; advertising to them will cost less than zero.

Change management like a Lego box

Last summer I met Håkan Lans, who is considered one of the greatest inventors of our time with inventions such as the colour graphics used in computers. Håkan told me that many of the successful inventors he knows have one thing in common from their childhoods – their mothers, from an early age, gave them toys without any given function. The toys forced them to make up what they were to be used for. Many toys, especially today, are often pre-packaged with a very specific function such as building a very specific house. When Håkan was young, Lego was just a box full of square blocks and possibilities. So I hope this book will be for you – full of possibilities. Regardless of whether you are a consumer or work in advertising, PR, R&D or top management, I hope you will be inspired to build innovations that will move your business forward and drag top management along with you.

The customers are getting smarter, but what about the companies?

Stupid advertising doesn't work with smart consumers. Liars don't build genuine relationships and with collective consumers, you can lie to one and the rest will know about it instantly. Think about it. The truth will set your brand free!

Follow the money into the future

When I look for motivation in business I often start by following the money. Why? Because in business people tend to do what makes them money. The same goes for both advertising and PR and any combination of them. The problem is to find out who is making money and why. Is it the agency, the client or the consumer? I believe that we need to have winners in all steps of the food chain. More products and services will be sold or recommended from consumers to consumers, and consumers are seeing that they contribute to business so they want their share of the money. Corporations are now starting to pay consumers to consume.

I don't think it's enough. I think we face a new economic time where money is not good enough as a value exchanger. Is money not an out-of-date model of putting a value on products and services? As Chris Anderson pointed out in his lecture: "Free is the price you have to pay to get consumers to start using your product and services." Corporations such as Microsoft built their empire on the free formula. That's the reason why they did not stop the piracy of their software in China (people got used to Windows). Now they are in many ways out compared by a more interesting free formula: Open Source. I think the reason is that if consumers can create something together they like it more and it will spread faster. Advertising can and will be the motivator to inspire consumers to get involved.

Consumers are contributing with their time, feedback and spreading the world – is that not worth more than money? This book is built on points, not pages, and it will continue for free on my blog: DetectiveMarketing.com. If you like this book, spread the word. (If you don't like this book, I've just wasted more than 2 years writing it.)

About the author

Author, consultant, and speaker Stefan Engeseth works and lectures internationally, but is based in Stockholm, Sweden. Over the years, Stefan has worked as a consultant for international and Fortune 500 corporations. He is often described as one of the world's leading experts and speakers in his field. His ideas range from innovative and future-oriented to bordering on far-fetched.

Yet, they all build on the universal truth that without innovation and vision, companies will not grow in today's highly competitive business world. The question is how far you are prepared to go. Stefan Engeseth is the founder and CEO of Detective Marketing™ a consulting firm that helps companies around the world find new business opportunities in areas such as strategy, business development and branding, communications, and marketing. He is also a creative advisor to a number of environmental and charitable organizations.

Stefan has previously written two books, *Detective Marketing*, and *ONE – A Consumer Revolution for Business* and contributes regularly to a number of business magazines. For more information about his books, speeches, consulting, or blog go to DetectiveMarketing.com.

Reading list

Anderson, 2006. *The Long Tail: Why the Future of Business is Selling Less of More.* Hyperion.

Anderson, 2008. *"Free! Why $0.00 Is the Future of Business"* Wired Magazine: Issue 16.03 (25 February 2008). *FREE,* 2009. Hyperion.

Balter, 2008. *The Word of Mouth Manual: Volume II.* Bzz Pubs.

Bauer, 2007. *Varför jag känner som du känner: intuitiv kommunikaton och hemligheten med spegelneuronerna.* Natur och Kultur.

Berger, 2004. *Advertising Today.* Phaidon Press.

Bono, 2007. *H+ (Plus) A New Religion?: How to Live Your Life Positively Through Happiness, Humour, Help, Hope, Health.* Ebury Press.

Brown, 2008. *Plan B 3.0: Mobilizing to Save Civilization (Third Edition).* W. W. Norton.

Chip/Heath, 2007. *Made to Stick: Why Some Ideas Survive and Others Die.* Random House.

Engeseth, 2006. *ONE: A Consumer Revolution for Business.* Marshall Cavendish and Cyan Books.

Engeseth, 2007. *Detective Marketing* (fourth edition). Engeseth Publishing.

Fallon/Senn, 2006. *Juicing the Orange: How to Turn Creativity into a Powerful Business Advantage.* Harvard Business School Press.

Freiberg/Freiberg, 2001. *Nuts! Southwest Airlines' Crazy Recipe for Business and Personal Success.* Thomson.

Gilbert, 2007. *Eat, Pray, Love.* Penguin.

Gladwell, 2002. *The Tipping Point: How Little Things Can Make a Big Difference.* Back Bay Books.

Gladwell, 2007. *Blink: The Power of Thinking Without Thinking.* Back Bay Books.

Godin, 2002. *Purple Cow: Transform Your Business by Being Remarkable.* Penguin Books.

Godin, 2008. *Tribes: We Need You to Lead Us.* Portfolio.

Gummesson, 2008. *Total Relationship Marketing* (third edition). Butterworth-Heinemann.

InternetWorld, 2008. Article: *Locket av för sociala medier.* Issue nr 5.

Jantsch, 2008. *Duct Tape Marketing*. Nelson Business.

Johnson, 2004. *Don't Think Pink*. Amacom.

Larsson, 2009. Article by Magnus Larsson, in Plaza Magazine. Issue nr 1.

Lindstrom, 2005. *BRAND sense: Build Powerful Brands through Touch, Taste, Smell, Sight, and Sound*. Free Press.

McConnell/Huba, 2006. *Citizen Marketers: When People Are the Message*. Kaplan Business.

Michaels, 2008. *Doubt is their product: How industry's assault on science threatens your health*. Oxford University Press.

Milton, 1996. *Skate: 100 Years of Figure Skating*. Trafalgar Square Publishing.

Moore, 2002. *Crossing the Chasm*. Collins Business.

Moore, 2008. *Dealing with Darwin: How Great Companies Innovate at Every Phase of Their Evolution*. Portfolio Trade.

Neumeier, 2007. *Zag: The Number One Strategy of High-Performance Brands*. Peachpit Press.

Pearce, 2006. *The Last Generation*. Eden Project Books.

Pinker, 2003. *The Blank Slate: The Modern Denial of Human Nature*. Penguin.

Rasulzada, 2007. *Dissertation: Organizational creativity and psychological well-being. Contextual aspects on organizational creativity and psychological well-being from an open systems perspective*. Lund University.

Ridley, 1994. *The Red Queen: Sex and the Evolution of Human*. Penguin Books.

Ries, 2002. Al & Laura Ries. *The Fall of Advertising and the Rise of PR*. HarperCollins.

Ries/Trout, 2001. *Positioning: The Battle for Your Mind*. McGraw-Hill.

Simmons, 2004. *My Sister's a Barista*. Cyan Books.

Strid/Andréasson, 2007. *The Viking Manifesto*. Marshall Cavendish and Cyan Books.

Tolle, 2008. *A New Earth*. Penguin.

Interviews and lectures

Albrecht, 2008. CEO, Hans-Holger Albrecht, MTG. Panel members at media seminar Stockholm MediaWeek (May 7-8).

Almö, 2008. Interview with CEO, Patrik Almö, Parts of Sweden (February 27).

Anderson, 2009. Lecture by Chris Anderson. At Mediaevolution (February 4).

Arsenius, 2008. Interview with fashion expert, Anders Arsenius (Mars 3).

Authried, 2008. Interview with salesperson, Ingeborg Authried, NK Manlig Depå (January 30).

Blom, 2008. Interview with game expert, Peter Blom, Jadestone (May 28 & June 9).

Bryhn, 2008. Interview with CEO, Robert Bryhn, Ogilvy Advertising, Sweden (August 12).

Burén, 2008. Interview with CEO, Claës af Burén, Gyro International (April 28).

Burman, 2008. Interview with CEO, Pål Burman, Fairshopping.se (January 21).

Cardeña, 2008. Interview with Professor of Parapsychology, Etzel Cardeña, Lund University, Dept. of Psychology (January 3).

Cole, 2008. Keynote lecture by Director, Jeffrey Cole, Centre for the Digital Future. At media seminar Stockholm MediaWeek (May 7-8).

Dahlén, 2007. Interview with Professor, Micael Dahlén, Centre for Consumer Marketing, Stockholm School of Economics (November 1).

Ericson, 2008. Interview with President, Anders Ericson, The Association of Swedish Advertisers (February 8).

Friberg, 2007. Interview and lecture with Co-founder, Adam Friberg, Cheap Monday (September 13).

Ghatan, 2008. Interview with brain researche, Per Hamid Ghatan, Karolinska Institutet (January 23).

Gillberg, 2008. Creative Director, Christina Gillberg, Gyro International (February 20).

Grahn Brikell, 2008. President, Pia Grahn Brikell, Advertising Association of Sweden (February 11).

Gunolf, 2008. Interview with CEO, Sofie Gunolf, Indiska Magasinet (January 18).

Gustafsson, 2008. Interview with CEO, Håkan Gustafsson, Carat Nordic (May 26).

Hellström, 2007. Group Manager, Maria Hellström, Cap Gemini. Lecture at Tendensdagen (October 18).

Hellström, 2007. Senior Manager Public Relations, Max Hellström, Domestic Appliances & Personal Care, Nordic, Philips (December 12).

Hertz, 2008. Interview with CEO, Cecilia Hertz, Umbilical design (June 30).

Higson, 2007. Interview with John Higson (November 30).

Hjelmtorp, 2008. Interview with gamer Daniel Hjelmtorp (January 22).

Hoffstedt, 2008. Interview with Senior advisor, Stig Hoffstedt, Lowe Brindfors (February 5).

Honkamaa, 2008. CEO, Stina Honkamaa, Google Sweden. Panel members at media seminar Stockholm MediaWeek (May 7-8).

Ingvar, 2008. Lecture by Professor, Martin Ingvar, Medicine Cognitive Neurophysiology, Karolinska Hospital. Topic: "Varumärket i hjärnan" at SmurfitKappa customer seminar (May 22).

Jebsen, 2008. Interview with Partner, Pål Jebsen, JKL Group (January 28).

Johansson/Julhen, 2008. Interview with Per Julhen and Public relations, Gunnar Johansson, Grin (May 5).

Kampmann, 2008. Interview with Creative Director, Patrick Kampmann, Publicis Stockholm (February 6).

Karlsson, 2008. Interview with Marketing director, Andreas Karlsson, Luthman Scandinavia (July 23).

Kroon, 2008. Interview with Director of Business development, Magnus Kroon, Swedish Trade Federation (January 17).

Lans, 2008. Interview with inventor Håkan Lans (July 9).

Lederhausen, 2008. Interview with founder & CEO, Mats Lederhausen, Be-Cause. Former senior executive of McDonald's Corporation (Mars 12).

Lindquist, 2007. Personnel manager, Staffan Lindquist, IKEA Sweden. Lecture at Butiksdagen (November 15).

Lindqvist Hotz, 2008. Interview with Minister, Lindqvist Hotz, Church of
Sweden (January 1).

Miksche, 2008. Interview with CEO, Mattias Miksche, Stardoll.com
(January 16).

Mäkitalo, 2008. Interview with "the father of the mobile phone" Professor,
Östen Mäkitalo, KTH - Royal Institute of Technology (May 6).

Nyvang, 2008. Interview with Nordic Marketing Director, Jonas Nyvang,
MySpace.com (January 22).

Näf, 2008. Lecture by Eric Näf, Director of Product Innovation, Absolut
Spirits. Topic: "Varumärket i hjärnan" at SmurfitKappa customer seminar
(May 22).

Olsson, 2008. Interview with Marketing and Communications Manager,
Merci Olsson, Nobelprize.org (February 7 & 15).

Palm-Jensen, 2008. Interview with CEO, Matias Palm-Jensen, Farfar
(January 16 & 23).

Rehn, 2008. Lecture by Professor in innovation, Alf Rehn. At seminar
Tendensdagen (October 23).

Reuterskiöld, 2008. Interview with President, Marianne Reuterskiöld, The
Swedish Marketing Federation (March 31).

Riese, 2008. Interview with Marketing Director, Patrik Riese, GM Nordic
(June 16).

Rosenfeld, 2009. Lecture by Business Development Manager, Alan Rosenfeld,
Apple. Topic: Convergence of Media. At Guldägget in Stockholm, Sweden
(31 March).

Sidhom, 2008. Interview with Planning Director, Saher Sidhom, Great Works
(April 24).

Solberg, 2008. Interview with CEO & President, Mikael Solberg, RNB Retail
and Brands (January 30).

Sundqvist, 2007. Interview with CEO, Gabriel Sundqvist, Pronto
Communication (October 15).

Taubert, 2007. Email interview with Associate Director, External Business
Development, Kai Taubert, Procter & Gamble (July 27).

Tavakoli, 2008. Interview with CEO, Sorosh Tavakoli, VideoPlaza (Mars 27).

Thunström, 2008. Interview with CEO, Pär Thunström, CEO, Buzzador (October 10).

Tutssel, 2008. Global Chief Creative Officer, Mark Tutssel, Leo Burnett. Panel members at media seminar Eurobest (December 1-3).

Uggla, 2008. Head of Ogilvy PR, Maria Uggla, Ogilvy Public Relations Worldwide, Stockholm (February 7).

Wahlund, 2007. Professor of economics specializing in media, Richard Wahlund, Stockholm School of Economics (December 17).

Viladevall, 2008. Managing Director, Carlos Viladevall, Magic Touch. Lecture at Stockholm MediaWeek (May 8).

Wistam, 2008. Interview with CEO, Magnus Wistam, Grey Sthlm (February 13).

Wåreus 2008. Interview with CEO, Carl Wåreus, OMD (Mars 18).

Wästberg, 2008. Interview with General Director, Olle Wästberg, The Swedish Institute (February 1).

Östberg, 2008. Interview with Marketing Director, Riitta Östberg, Choice Hotels Sweden (February 15).

Online references

Adage.com, 2008. Article: Starbucks Sees Profits Drop 28% in Second Quarter,
by Emily Bryson York (May 1).

Adage.com, 2008. Article: TBWA Guru Lee Clow Says Online Branding Still
in Infancy, by Alice Z. Cuneo (April 29).

Afflictionclothing.com

Aftonbladet.se, 2004. Article: En hel butik – för singlar,
by Helena Gunnarsson (August 25).

Alexanderlervik.com

Algore.com

Americanapparel.net

Apple.com

Axbo.com

Bebo.com

Bemz.com

Bikefurniture.com

Blogcatalog.com

Bongo.com

Brandchannel.com, 2002. Article: The Sport of Naming,
by John Karolefski (May 13).

Brandchannel.com, 2003. Article: It may be past but it's not over,
by Michael Standaert (May 13).

Brandfame.com

Brucespringsteen.net

Cheapmonday.com

Cnet.com, 2005. Article: Google in San Francisco: 'Wireless overlord?',
by Elinor Mills (October 1).

Dn.se, 2008. Article: Tandlöst ledarskap på SVT slösar bort licenspengarna,
by Stina Dabrowski (August 10).

Dogsrule.com

Drphilstore.com

Earth.google.com

EBay.com

Eurobest.com

Facebook.com

Farfar.se

Fastcompany.com, 2009. Article: The Real Story Behind Bisphenol A,
by David Case (Jan 23).

Fender.com

Flickr.com

Fuh2.com

Gibson.com

Gm.com

Gmail.com

Google.com

Googleblog.blogspot.com, 2008. Blogpost: Be who you want on the Web pages
you visit, by Niniane Wang, Engineering Manager, Google.com (August 7).

Grin.se

Guitarhero.com

Honeywell.com

Iht.com, 2008. International Herald Tribune, 2008. Article:
Hamburg soccer fans get own cemetery (September 9).

IKEA.com

Indiatimes.com, 2008. Article: Net-savvy public chisel out their own opinions
on brands, by Venkatesh Rangachari (June 9).

Indiska.com

Intel.com

Ipa.co.uk, 2007. Report: Re-invention is key if agencies are to survive
(January 5).

Ireport.com

Jaiku.com

Junglejims.com

Leonardodicaprio.com

Linkedin.com

Markoff, 2005. Article: Google Bids to Help San Francisco Go Wireless,
     by John Markoff (October 1).

Meetup.com

Mitsubishisucks.com

Monster.com

Mtg.se

MTV.com

MySpace.com

Newsgator.com

Ning.com

Nobelprize.org

NudieJeans.com

Nytimes.com, 2007. Article: For $82 a Day, Booking a Cell in a 5-Star Jail,
     by Jennifer Steinhauer (April 29).

Oprah.com

Pacemaker.net

Partsofsweden.se

Paulpottsuk.com

Peopleowned.org

Pinkspage.com

Prisonlegalnews.org

Resume.se, 2007. Article: Thai Air ger rabatt i utbyte mot publicitet,
     by Leif Holmkvist (Oktober 2).

Scion.com

Secondlife.com

Signspotting.com

Singelringen.com

Socialthing.com

Sony.com

Spotify.com

Spychips.com

Stardoll.com

Tapout.com

Ted.com, 2004. Speech: What we can learn from spaghetti sauce,
by Malcolm Gladwell (February).

Ted.com, 2007. Speech: Predicting the next 5,000 days of the Web,
by Kevin Kelly (December).

Ted.com, 2008. Speech: Asking big questions about the universe, by Professor,
Stephen Hawking (February).

Tigerbalm.com

Tommytv.com

Triiibes.com

Tv.audi.com

Twingly.com

Twitter.com

Ufc.com

Wahlberg, 2005. Article: Hans-Holger Albrecht lämnar Metro,
by Maria Wahlberg (January 13).

Walmartmovie.com

Wecansolveit.org

Willebrand, 2007. Article: Cheap Monday breddar varumärket – utan reklam,
at Resume.se, by Peter Willebrand (August 15).

Wired.com, 2007. Article: Intel Launches a Digg to Rate Software Start-ups,
by Bryan Gardiner (August 10).

Worldofwarcraft.com

YouTube.com

Linked words

15 minutes of fame
http://en.Wikipedia.org/wiki/15_minutes_of_fame

American Idol
http://www.americanidol.com/

Andy Warhol
http://en.wikiquote.org/wiki/Andy_Warhol

Anthony Mills
http://www.myspace.com/ghettotrance

Ashton Kutcher
http://en.Wikipedia.org/wiki/Ashton_Kutcher

Avatar
http://en.Wikipedia.org/wiki/Avatar_%28virtual_reality%29

Bamble
http://www.bamble.kommune.no/

Barry White
http://en.wikipedia.org/wiki/Barry_White

Beetle
http://www.vw.com/newbeetle/en/us/

Biometrics
http://en.Wikipedia.org/wiki/Biometrics

Bobby Fischer
http://en.Wikipedia.org/wiki/Bobby_Fischer

Bond
http://en.Wikipedia.org/wiki/Human_bonding

Celebration
http://en.Wikipedia.org/wiki/Celebration,_Florida

Cosplay
http://en.Wikipedia.org/wiki/Cosplay

Counter-strike
http://en.Wikipedia.org/wiki/Counter-Strike

CSR - Corporate Social Responsibility
http://en.Wikipedia.org/wiki/Corporate_social_responsibility

Darth Vader
http://en.wikipedia.org/wiki/Darth_Vader

Dana White
http://en.Wikipedia.org/wiki/Dana_White

Debriefing
http://en.Wikipedia.org/wiki/Debriefing

DJ – Disc jockey
http://en.Wikipedia.org/wiki/Disc_jockey

Dodge La Femme
http://en.Wikipedia.org/wiki/Dodge_La_Femme

Framing
http://en.Wikipedia.org/wiki/Framing_(social_sciences)

Gateway of India
http://www.mumbainet.com/travel/gateway.htm

Georges St. Pierre
http://en.Wikipedia.org/wiki/Georges_St._Pierre

GPS – Global Positioning System
http://en.Wikipedia.org/wiki/Global_Positioning_System

Great white shark
http://en.Wikipedia.org/wiki/Great_white_shark

Greenwash
http://en.Wikipedia.org/wiki/Greenwash

Half-Life
http://en.wikipedia.org/wiki/Half-Life_(series)

Heidi Klum
http://en.Wikipedia.org/wiki/Heidi_Klum

Hilton
http://en.Wikipedia.org/wiki/Hilton_Hotels_Corporation

Hooligans
http://en.Wikipedia.org/wiki/Football_hooliganism

Humburg SV
http://en.Wikipedia.org/wiki/Hamburger_SV

Håkan Lans
http://en.Wikipedia.org/wiki/H%C3%A5kan_Lans

Ingvar Kamprad
http://en.Wikipedia.org/wiki/Ingvar_Kamprad

Jimi Hendrix
www.jimi-hendrix.com

K-1
http://en.Wikipedia.org/wiki/K-1

Kevin Kelly
www.kk.org

Madison Square Garden
http://www.Wikipedia.org/wiki/Madison_Square_Garden

Madonna
http://en.wikipedia.org/wiki/Madonna_(entertainer)

Maslow's
http://en.wikipedia.org/wiki/Maslow%27s_hierarchy_of_needs

MBA
http://en.wikipedia.org/wiki/Master_of_Business_Administration

Minute Maid Park
http://www.Wikipedia.org/wiki/Minute_Maid_Park

Mirror neurons
http://en.Wikipedia.org/wiki/Mirror_neuron

MMA
http://en.wikipedia.org/wiki/Mixed_martial_arts

Mod
http://en.Wikipedia.org/wiki/Mod_%28computer_gaming%29

Nicknames
http://www.Wikipedia.org/wiki/Nickname

OS 2008 Beijing
http://en.beijing2008.cn/

Paris Hilton
http://en.Wikipedia.org/wiki/Paris_Hilton

Paul Potts 2007
http://en.Wikipedia.org/wiki/Paul_Potts#Britain.27s_Got_Talent

Podcast
http://en.Wikipedia.org/wiki/Podcast

Punk'd
http://en.wikipedia.org/wiki/Punk%27d

Randy Couture
http://www.thenatural.tv

Robot dog
http://en.wikipedia.org/wiki/Aibo

Rock Band
http://en.Wikipedia.org/wiki/Rock_Band_(video_game)

RSS - Really Simple Syndication
http://en.Wikipedia.org/wiki/RSS_(file_format)

Saab 92001
http://en.wikipedia.org/wiki/Saab_92001

Sigmund Freud
http://en.Wikipedia.org/wiki/Sigmund_Freud

Space tourism
http://en.wikipedia.org/wiki/Space_tourism

Spencer Tunick
http://en.wikipedia.org/wiki/Spencer_Tunick

St. Bernard dog
http://en.wikipedia.org/wiki/St._Bernard_(dog)

Tamara Gielen
http://www.b2bemailmarketing.com/2007/02/speaking_at_a_s.html

Tila Nguyen
http://en.Wikipedia.org/wiki/Tila_Tequila

Tonya Harding
http://en.Wikipedia.org/wiki/Tonya_Harding

We take no responsibility for keeping these links up-to-date
(or for the content).

Movies

An Inconvenient Truth, directed by Davis Guggenheim, 2006.

Crazy People, directed by Tony Bill, 1990.

Jerry Maguire, directed by Cameron Crowe, 1996.

Sicko, directed by, Michael Moore, 2007.

Super Size Me, directed by Morgan Spurlock, 2004.

The 11th Hour, directed by Nadia Conners and Leila Conners Petersen, 2007.

The Corporation, directed by Mark Achbar, 2003.

The Great Global Warming Swindle, directed by Martin Durkin, 2007.

The Simpsons, 1989–

Wal-Mart: The High Cost of Low Price, directed by Robert Greenwald, 2005.

Acknowledgements

First of all, I would like to thank Al Ries for believing in me and for giving me permission to use our email conversation as the foreword for this book. My family (including everything in the universe). My girlfriend. As a dyslexic writer, I have found it invaluable to work with Steve Strid, who has translated my sometimes cryptic scribbling into intelligible words. Proofreading and editing by Ken Neptune. Roland Williams for his talented illustrations. My super-mentor, Claes Andréasson, always ready to share his experience and advice. My friend and colleague Per Nilsson. Carin Balfe Arbman, Partner, Re: Public Relations. Al Gore. Jörgen Wahl. Seth Godin. Chief Oren Lyons. Joachim Nordwall, designer, Jnordwall.com. Hero, Jack Yan. Igor Polyakov, Creative Director, Hot Snow. Dallas. Rosengård. Söder. Erik Dahlberg. Stuart Pledger. Jan Cederquist. Fredrik Wackå. Jonas Nilsson. Bengt Jönsson. Maria Forssén. Stefan Broman. Annette Sandgren. Yann Mauchamp. Walter. Glenn Lundberg. Anna Caracolias. Mattias Durnik. Manoj. Daniel Hjelmtorp. Rupert Steiner. Charlotte Wik. Jack Hansen. Ib. John. The Huldt-Ramberg family in Regina. The Gregerman and Björkholtz families. Sergej. The Petrovski families. Professor Evert Gummesson. OnTime. Strålfors. Big thanks to designer Alexander Lervik and Johan Wahlbäck, founder of Singelringen.com, for your talent and permission to use your visual material. Norhaven. Holmen Paper. Iggesund Paperboard.

Special thanks to everyone I have interviewed for this book. You have really given me inspiration and kept me young and hungry to keep learning new things: Patrik Riese, Marketing Director, GM Nordic. Anders Ericson, President, The Association of Swedish Advertisers. Pia Grahn Brikell, President, Advertising Association of Sweden. Mariann Eriksson, Director of Communications, WWF-Sweden. Maria Uggla, Head of Ogilvy PR, Ogilvy Public Relations Worldwide. Peter Blom, Gaming Expert, Jadestone. Fashion Expert, Anders Arsenius. Professor Östen Mäkitalo, KTH - Royal Institute of Technology. Professor Micael Dahlén,

Center for Consumer Marketing, Stockholm School of Economics. Cecilia Hertz, CEO, Umbilical Design. John Higson. Alf Rehn, Professor in Innovation. Riitta Östberg, Marketing Manager, Choice Hotels Sweden AB. Jan Fager, President and Marianne Reuterskiöld, former President, The Swedish Marketing Federation. Mats Lederhausen, Founder & CEO, Be-Cause. Ewa Lindqvist Hotz, Minister in the Church of Sweden. Mikael Solberg, CEO & President, RNB Retail and Brands. Ingeborg Authried, Salesperson, NK Manlig Depå. Kai Taubert, Associate Director External Business Development, Procter & Gamble. Olle Wästberg, General Director, The Swedish Institute. Saher Sidhom, Planning Director, Great Works. Per Hamid Ghatan, Brain Researcher, Karolinska Institutet. Claës af Burén, CEO and Creative Director, Christina Gillberg, Gyro International. Carl Wåreus, CEO, OMD. Merci Olsson, Marketing and Communications Manager, Nobelprize.org. Richard Wahlund, Professor, Stockholm School of Economics. Patrik Almö, CEO, Parts of Sweden. Sorosh Tavakoli, CEO, VideoPlaza. Max Hellström, Senior Manager Public Relations, Domestic Appliances & Personal Care, Nordic, Philips. Pål Jebsen, Partner, JKL Group. Professor of Parapsychology, Etzel Cardeña, Lund University, Psychology of Dept. Håkan Gustafsson, CEO, Carat Nordic. Magnus Wistam, CEO, Grey Sthlm. Gamer, Daniel Hjelmtorp. Stig Hoffstedt, Senior advisor, Lowe Brindfors. Robert Bryhn, CEO, Ogilvy Advertising, Sweden. Patrick Kampmann, Creative Director, Publicis Stockholm. Riitta Östberg, Marketing Director, Choice Hotels Sweden. Patrik Almö, CEO, Parts of Sweden. Håkan Lans. Richard Wahlund, Professor of Economics (specialized in media), Stockholm School of Economics. Per Julhen and Public Relations, Gunnar Johansson, Grin. Magnus Kroon, Director of Business Development, Swedish Trade Federation. Sofie Gunolf, CEO, Indiska Magasinet. Jonas Nyvang, Nordic Marketing Director, MySpace.com. Matias Palm-Jensen, CEO, Farfar. Mattias Miksche, CEO, Stardoll.com. Andreas Karlsson, Marketing Director, Luthman Scandinavia. Adam Friberg, Co-founder, Cheap Monday. Gabriel Sundqvist, CEO, Pronto Communication. Pål Burman, CEO, Fairshopping.se. CEO, Pär Thunström, CEO, Buzzador.

Kurt Svantesson, Business Director, AGA Consumer. Forsman & Bodenfors. Johnnie Moore. Nilgun & Ulf Carlson. Thanks to all clients, people, lectures, books, the Internet and the other 3,567,879 things in the universe that have inspired me over the years. All trademarks in this book are acknowledged as belonging to their respective companies.

Most of all, I would like to thank you for taking the time to read this book, and if you like it, spread the word!

Index

Also available

ISBN: 978-91-633-0375-3

Praise for Detective Marketing

"Some really good examples of business metaphors"
TOM PETERS!

"Swedish business bible."
Brand Strategy

"Detective Marketing is one of the best books to spotlight how become creative in the marketing process."
Anders Ericson, President, The Association of
Swedish Advertisers

"Amusing case studies..."
Brandchannel.com

"Engeseth is brilliantly witty."
Asia-Inc Magazine

"Engeseth's ideas are radical 2000s' evolution."
All About Branding

"Engeseth offers suggestions for increasing your creativity."
The Chicago Sun-Times

"Don't highlight while reading . . . or the pages in this enlightening little book will be wet with color. Instead of searching for insights in the thousands of books on marketing, branding and innovation, simply read - and reread this one. And then use those insights to grow your brand and to make a difference in other people's lives."
Tom Asacker, Author of Sandbox Wisdom

.... pearls of wisdom are available at DetectiveMarketing
Design Week

"This book lets me travel from imagination to practical experience."
Jörgen Wahl, CEO, AdvisoryBoard

Also available

First published in 2006. Second edition published in 2008.
Publisher: Marshall Cavendish
ISBN 978-0-462-09941-5

Praise for ONE

"...ONE is the ultimate consumer book."
> Al Ries, Advertising Age top 10 business guru
> and bestselling author

"In our brave new opt-in, on-demand world, consumers possess ultimate control over how, when and what messages are received. Stefan Engeseth's provocative new book smartly explains how businesses can effectively tap into the consumer revolution – instead of being overthrown by it."
> O. Burtch Drake, former President and CEO,
> American Association of Advertising Agencies

"Engeseth's latest book ONE once again makes us realize why the consumer is the king!"
> Martin Lindstrom, branding consultant and
> author of Brandchild and Brand Sense

"ONE is the only way for marketing to go. Without a close communion with customers, companies are just guessing what people want. If managers want a real dialogue, Engeseth's book is an essential read."
> Nicholas Ind, author of Living the Brand
> and Inspiration

"If you buy one business book this year, buy ONE."
> Stephen Brown, Professor of Marketing Research,
> University of Ulster

"Using simple, yet thought-provoking examples, Stefan Engeseth manages to inspire both creativity and clear-sightedness."
> Claes Andreasson, former director of Absolut
> Akademi, the ABSOLUT Company